CONTENTS

1)	Introduction to Charles Dickens	1
2)	Inctroduction to Oliver Twist	11
3)	Textual Analysis	17
	Chapters 1 - 15	17
	Chapters 16 - 28	34
	Chapters 29 - 38	54
	Chapters 39 - 53	68
4)	Character Analyses	87
5)	Critical Commentary	99
6)	Essay Questions and Answers	106
7)	Bibliography	112

BRIGHT NOTES

OLIVER TWIST BY CHARLES DICKENS

Intelligent Education

Nashville, Tennessee

BRIGHT NOTES: Oliver Twist
www.BrightNotes.com

No part of this publication may be used or reproduced in any manner whatsoever without written permission, except in the case of brief quotations in critical articles and reviews. For permissions, contact Influence Publishers http://www.influencepublishers.com.

ISBN: 978-1-645420-58-3 (Paperback)
ISBN: 978-1-645420-59-0 (eBook)

Published in accordance with the U.S. Copyright Office Orphan Works and Mass Digitization report of the register of copyrights, June 2015.

Originally published by Monarch Press.
Edward R. Winans, 1966
2020 Edition published by Influence Publishers.

Interior design by Lapiz Digital Services. Cover Design by Thinkpen Designs.

Printed in the United States of America.

Library of Congress Cataloging-in-Publication Data forthcoming.
Names: Intelligent Education
Title: BRIGHT NOTES: Oliver Twist
Subject: STU004000 STUDY AIDS / Book Notes

CHARLES DICKENS

INTRODUCTION

EARLY LIFE

Charles Dickens was born on February 7, 1812, in Portsea. His father, John Dickens, was a minor clerk in the Navy Pay Office; his father's parents had been servants and his mother's parents only slightly higher on the social scale. John Dickens was a happy-go-lucky, improvident man whose family often knew want as the debts piled up. At the age of twelve, Charles Dickens experienced what was to become the key event of his life. His father was imprisoned for debt in the Marshalsea Prison; young Charles was taken out of school and put to work in a blacking warehouse in London, pasting labels on bottles of shoe polish. Although he later returned to school for a time, this experience left a permanent mark on the soul of Charles Dickens. Even many years later, after he had become a successful author, he could not bear to talk about it, or be reminded of his family's ignominy.

At the age of fifteen Dickens began working as an office boy for a law firm. He taught himself shorthand and by 1828 he became a reporter for the lay courts of Doctors' Common. The dull routine of the legal profession never interested him, so he became a newspaper reporter for the *Mirror of Parliament*, *The True Sun*, and finally for the *Morning Chronicle*. (John Forster, later his closest friend and biographer, was also employed at *The True Sun*.) By the age of twenty, Dickens was one of the best Parliamentary reporters in all England.

During this same period Dickens' interest began to switch from journalism to literature. His first work of fiction, "Dinner at Poplar Walk" (later reprinted as "Mr. Minns and His Cousin"), appeared in the *Monthly Magazine* when he was twenty-one. His newspaper work had given him an intimate knowledge of the streets and byways of London, and late in 1832 he began writing sketches and stories of London life. They began to appear in periodicals and newspapers in 1833, and in 1836 were gathered together as *Sketches by Boz, Illustrations of Every-day Life, and Every-day People*. This pseudonym, Boz, was suggested by his brother's pronunciation of "Moses" when he had a cold.

PICKWICK PAPERS

The success of the Sketches brought an invitation from the publishers Chapman and Hall in 1836 to furnish the "letter-press" for a series of cartoon sketches about a humorous cockney sporting club. (The letter-press was little more than a running accompaniment, like an ornamental border around the drawings.) The project had hardly begun when Robert Seymour, the artist, committed suicide. Dickens searched long for a new artist and found an ideal collaborator in H. K. Browne ("Phiz"), but Dickens had persuaded the publisher to let him improvise a fictional narrative. When the *Posthumous Papers of the Pickwick Club* finally came out, the story predominated over the illustrations.

When *Pickwick Papers* appeared in April, 1836, as a monthly serial, the sales were at first discouraging. Of the first issue, a modest 400 copies were printed; later the work became increasingly popular. Some 40,000 copies of each issue were sold. After the last installment appeared in November, 1837, the novel was published in book form. This set the pattern for all of Dickens' subsequent novels.

The success of *Pickwick* convinced Dickens that his real career lay in writing fiction; he gave up his Parliamentary reporting in order to devote himself full time to it. In 1836 he had married Catherine Hogarth, the daughter of one of the owners of the *Morning Chronicle*; his growing family made it necessary to work exhaustingly at his writing. His next work, *Oliver Twist*, began appearing even before *Pickwick* was completed. Nicholas Nickleby followed in a like manner in 1838-39, and the very first number sold some 50,000 copies. During this same period he was editor of *Bentley's Miscellany* (1837-39). By the 1840s Dickens had become the most popular novelist in Britain, taking over the place long held by Sir Walter Scott.

THE MIDDLE YEARS

The years between 1840 and 1855 were most fruitful ones: *The Old Curiosity Shop*, *Barnaby Rudge*, *A Christmas Carol*, *Martin Chuzzlewit*, *Dombey and Son*, *David Copperfield*, *Bleak House*, *Little Dorritt*, and *Hard Times* all appeared. In addition, he made his first trip to America; copyright laws at that time allowed American publishers to pirate his works, and their lack of concern over this injustice undoubtedly contributed to Dickens' unfavorable criticism of America in *Martin Chuzzlewit*. In 1850 Dickens founded his own periodical, *Household Words*, and continued to edit it until he and his partner exchanged it for

All the Year Round in 1859. *Hard Times, A Tale of Two Cities*, and *Great Expectations* appeared in serial form in these publications. But these years of literary success were marred by domestic strife. He and his wife had never been particularly suited to each other, and their marriage ended in separation in 1856.

In addition to writing, Dickens had another love - amateur theatricals - which led him into yet another pursuit in the latter part of his career. He gave public readings from his novels from 1859 to 1868 in England, Scotland, and America. He had always loved the theater - he studied drama as a young man and had organized an amateur theatrical company of his own in 1847 (he was both manager and principal actor).

His energies never seemed to fail: he burned the candle at both ends. He published *Our Mutual Friend* in 1864 - 65 and at his death left an unfinished novel, *The Mystery of Edwin Drood*, a suspense tale in the nature of a detective story. He died suddenly in 1870 from a stroke at the age of fifty-eight. G. K. Chesterton once said that Dickens died of "popularity." It would seem so; his exhaustive burden (marked by insomnia and fatigue) is well catalogued in his letters. He was buried in the Poets' Corner of Westminster Abbey.

Dickens wrote with an eye on the tastes of a wide readership, never far ahead of the printer, and was always ready to modify the story to suit his readers. For example, when the sales of serial installments of *Martin Chuzzlewit* fell from 60,000 to 20,000, Dickens sent his hero off to America in order to stimulate renewed interest. No novelist ever had so close a relationship with his public, a public ranging from barely literate factory girls to wealthy dowagers, but consisting mostly of the newly formed middle classes.

TEACHER AND ENTERTAINER

Walter Allen in *The English Novel* points out that Dickens became the spokesman for this rising middle class, and also its teacher. "Dickens more than any of his contemporaries was the expression of the conscience-untutored, baffled, muddled as it doubtless often was-of his age," he writes. Not only in his novels, but in his magazine, *Household Words*, Dickens lashed out at what he considered the worst social abuses of his time: imprisonment for debt, the ferocious penal code, the unsanitary slums which bred criminals, child labor, the widespread mistreatment of children, the unsafe machinery in factories, and the hideous schools.

Yet, as Allen suggests, Dickens was primarily a great entertainer, "the greatest entertainer, probably, in the history of fiction." It is significant that Dickens was not satisfied to have his books the best sellers of their time. He wanted to see his audience, to manipulate it with the power of his own words. His public readings gave him an excellent opportunity to do so. Sitting alone on a bare stage, he would read excerpts from various novels, act them out really, imitating the voices of the various characters. These theatrical readings would always contain a dying-child scene or two which left his audience limp and tear-stained. Dickens suffered all the emotions with his audience, even after repeated readings, and this undoubtedly helped to shorten his life. He entertained his readers with humor, pathos, suspense, and melodrama, all on a grand scale. Charles Dickens had a fertile imagination that peopled his novels with characters and events which continue to entertain twentieth-century readers as they delighted his contemporaries.

NOVEL TECHNIQUE

An understanding of Dickens as an artist requires an understanding of the method of publication he used-monthly or weekly installments. Serialization left its mark on his fiction and often accounts for the flaws which many critics have found in his work. John Butt and Kathleen Tillotson in *Dickens at Work* (1957) describe the problems serial publication imposed:

"Chapters must be balanced within a number in respect both of length and of effect. Each number must lead, if not to a **climax**, at least to a point of rest; and the rest between numbers is necessarily more extended than what the mere chapter divisions provide. The writer had also to bear in mind that his readers were constantly interrupted for prolonged periods, and that he must take this into account in his characterizations and, to some extent, in his plotting."

This technique brought on a loose, episodic treatment with a vast, intricate plot, numerous characters and much repetition to jog the reader's memory. Instead of the whole novel slowly building to a real **climax**, each part had to have a little **climax** of its own. In *Hard Times* the bad effects of serialization are at a minimum because it is a comparatively short novel (about 260 pages in most editions) and it appeared in weekly rather than monthly parts. But the careful reader can still tell where each part ended; considerations of space rather than of artistic technique formed the story.

The works of Dickens have many of their roots in the eighteenth century, especially in the novels of Tobias Smollett, whom he greatly admired. From Smollett he borrowed many devices of characterization - "tagging" characters with physical peculiarities, speech mannerisms, compulsive gestures, and eccentric names. Examples in *Hard Times* include the distinctive speech pattern of Stephen Blackpool, who talks in a phonetically transcribed Lancashire dialect; the self-deprecating speech of Bounderby or the self-pitying talk of Mrs. Sparsit; the physical peculiarities of Bitzer, the epitome of pallidness; the names of characters - Bounderby, M'Choakumchild, Gradgrind-so evocative of their personalities.

The eighteenth century also brought the picaresque tradition in fiction to full flower. (The term refers to novels which depict the life of a picaro [Spanish: "rogue"] and which consist of unconnected **episodes** held together by the presence of the central character.) Early novels, especially those of Defoe, Fielding, and Smollett, were rambling, episodic, and anecdotal. Many of the novels of Dickens– *Pickwick, Oliver Twist, David Copperfield* to name a few - are picaresque in technique. *Hard Times* borrows from the tradition only the irreverent, satirical view of stuffed-shirt pretentiousness and of established society in general. The eighteenth-century theater, with its sharply defined villains, its involved melodramatic plots, and its farcical humor, also suggested ideas for plots and characterizations to Dickens.

Dickens took his descriptive techniques from Sir Walter Scott and other early nineteenth-century novelists. No character, no matter how minor, appears on the scene without being fully described, not only as to physical appearance, but as to the clothing he wears. Dickens also excels in the short but evocative description of places; in *Hard Times* note the portrayal of the murky streets and factories of Coketown and of its blighted wasteland-like countryside.

THE WORLD OF HIS NOVELS

The world of Dickens' novels is a fantasy world, a fairy-tale world, a nightmare world. It is a world seen as through the eyes of a child: the shadows are blacker, the fog denser, the houses higher, the midnight streets emptier and more terrifying than in reality. To a child, inanimate objects have lives of their own: thus the smoke malevolently winds over Coketown like serpents and the pistons of the steam engines in the factory are "melancholy mad elephants."

The characters, too, are seen as children see people. Their peculiarities are heightened to eccentricities; their vices, to monstrous proportions. Most of the people in his novels are caricatures, characterized by their externals, almost totally predictable in behavior. We know little about them beyond their surface behavior; Dickens focuses on the outward man, not the inner motives. It is interesting to note, however, that Dickens was able to create intensely individual portraits even though he lacked the ability to analyze motivation and character developments. His characters are more than types or mere abstract representations of virtue or vice. They are intensely alive and thus memorable. The characters from a Dickens novel are remembered long after the plots and even the titles of the books have been forgotten.

DICKENS THE REFORMER

Dickens in his lifetime saw Great Britain change from a rural, agricultural "Merrie Old England" of inns, stagecoaches, and fox-hunting squires to an urbanized, commercial-industrial land of railroads, factories, slums, and a city proletariat. These changes are chronicled in his novels, and it is possible to read them as a social history of England. *Pickwick*, although set in 1827-28, reflects much of what still survived of the old eighteenth-century way of life. *Oliver Twist* (1837-39) shows the first impact of the Industrial Revolution - the poverty existing at that time and the feeble attempt to remedy it by workhouses. *Dombey and Son* (1846-48) describes the coming of the railroad, a symbol of change. Dombey, the merchant, sacrifices love, wife, and children for a position of power through money; yet he is already obsolete, for the industrialist is the ruler now.

Dickens grew increasingly bitter with each novel; his criticism of society became more radical, his **satire** more biting and less sweetened by humor. In his later novels he often broke out in indignant exasperation and almost hysterical anger. He figuratively mounted a soapbox, demanding that the "Lords and Gentlemen" do something about the appalling conditions of the poor.

In his early novels, society itself is not evil; it is only some people who are bad and who create misery for others by their callousness and neglect. By the time of *Dombey and Son* it is institutions which are evil, representing in that novel the self-expanding power of accumulated money. *Bleak House* (1852-53) attacks the law's delay and the self-perpetuating mass of futility it has become. *Hard Times* (1854) savagely lampoons the economic theories which Dickens considered responsible for much of human misery. The English historian, Lord Macaulay, charged that it was full of "sullen Socialism." Of *Little Dorritt* (1855-57), which attacks prisons and imprisonment for debt, George Bernard Shaw said that it was "more seditious than Karl Marx." In *Our Mutual Friend* (1864-65) we see the fully disillusioned Dickens. The atmosphere of the novel is grim, permeated with a sense of growing nightmare. There is the feeling that something deep and basic is wrong with the social order, something beyond the mere reforming of bad people or poorly-run institutions.

T. A. Jackson in *Charles Dickens: The Progress of a Radical* tries to claim him for the Marxists as a champion of the downtrodden masses. Yet Lenin, the father of Communist Russia, found Dickens intolerable in his "middle class sentimentality." George Orwell was probably correct when he stated that Dickens' criticism of society was neither political nor economic, but moral. Certainly Dickens offered no substitutes for the system or institutions he attacked. Thus in *A Tale of Two Cities* (1859) he expressed his loathing for the decadent French aristocracy of the ancient regime, but he seemed to like the triumphant democracy of the Revolution no better. In *Hard Times* he excoriates the exploitation of the industrial workers by the factory owners, but he is repelled almost equally by the attempt of the workers to form unions in self-defense. He seems to suggest that the Golden Rule is the only solution to class struggle.

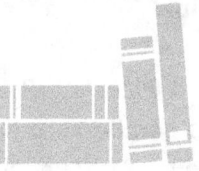

OLIVER TWIST

INTRODUCTION

The Adventures of Oliver Twist was first published under the title of *Oliver Twist: or the Parish Boy's Progress*, by "Boz" in three volumes in 1838. It ran as a serial in the pages of *Bentley's Miscellany* from January 1837 to April 1839, and was issued in ten monthly parts from January to October 1846. Dickens was himself editor of *Bentley's Miscellany* from 1837 to 1839. He had signed a contract with Richard Bentley, the publisher, for three novels. Unfortunately, although he was enormously popular with the public and his books a financial success, Dickens did not reap the benefits. Bentley, a poor businessman, did not have the foresight to adjust his contract with Dickens and thus lost a great potential profit to the publishers Chapman and Hall who took over Dickens' work. While writing *Oliver Twist*, Dickens wrote to John Forster (later his biographer) in January 1839: "... the consciousness that my books are enriching everybody connected with them but myself, and that I, with such a popularity as I have acquired, am struggling in old toils, and wasting my energies in the very height and freshness of my fame, and the best part of my life, to fill the pockets of others, while for those who are nearest and dearest to me I can realize little more than a genteel subsistence: all this puts me out of heart and spirits...."

Oliver Twist followed *Pickwick Papers*, one of the jolliest books ever written; its somber atmosphere stands in sharp contrast to the earlier novel. Although his second novel retained some of the farcical humor (see Giles and Brittles), it struck a new and darker note. Its focus is the miserable reality of poverty and crime in early Victorian England: it is intensely topical to the time of its publication. In making Saffron Hill the central scene of *Oliver Twist*, Dickens was using a contemporary setting which a great number of his readers knew well. Its reputation was notorious. Schools for young thieves, like Fagin's, continued for many years.

One of the central points of Dickens' attack on social abuses was the new Poor Law, introduced in 1834 as an attempt to discourage pauperism. It was a harsh system, based on the idea that poverty was a crime. Its guiding rule was that poor relief should be granted only to able-bodied poor and their dependents in well-regulated workhouses under conditions inferior to those of the humblest laborers outside. Families were often split up, or sent to workhouses; there were rigid dietary prescriptions - Dickens' "three meals of thin gruel a day, with an onion twice a week, and half a roll on Sundays" was an exaggeration, but it had quite an effect on the English reading public when Oliver "asked for more." The extremely severe winter of 1837-38, the high price of corn, trade depression, and unemployment made the Poor Law even more unpopular than it had been before. A novel could hardly have been more topical than *Oliver Twist*: the season made it a foregone conclusion.

Dickens concentrated his attack on the bad workhouse feeding, the absurdity of such officers as Bumble and the utter failure to make any proper provision for pauper children. He also criticized the legal system which deprived the poor of the right to a proper defense (see Oliver's trial in **Chapter Eleven**). The state of affairs described in the opening chapters of *Oliver Twist* continued substantially unaltered for many years after the book was published, but the authorities were never immune from criticism and made ineffectual attempts to meet it. Dickens undoubtedly played a significant role in jogging the slow processes of administrative muddle and neglect.

In addition to using the contemporary scene as background for his novel, he drew heavily on personal experience. Dickens, himself a product of that class of Victorian society called "shabby gentility," utilized his own firsthand experiences with poverty and his experiences as a reporter to vividly and accurately portray the seamy side of London society. No writer, before or since, knew so intimately the London of the poor and the underworld. Needless to say, the novel shocked Victorians, many of whom refused to believe that such people as appeared in these pages really existed. But if we are to believe the reports of Dickens' contemporaries as to the truth of his portrayals, and Dickens' defense which appeared as a Preface to the 1841 edition of *Oliver Twist*, they did exist.

Dickens borrowed the name Fagin from Bob Fagin a boy who had befriended him during his unfortunate experience in the blacking warehouse, but Mr. Fang, the magistrate, is a portrait of Mr. Laing, a real magistrate whom Dickens had observed. And so, with his second novel (*Sketches by Boz* was a collection of unrelated short pieces), Dickens began in earnest to explore the dark side of an era in which the British Empire grew to greatness, but was slow to utilize the wealth and power which that great expansion brought to alleviate the poverty and misery within. And although nowhere did Dickens offer anything like a political or economic solution, his brilliant and imaginative portrait illuminated the problems so that other men could.

In a certain sense, *Oliver Twist* is more an allegorical fairy tale than a novel. It is much closer to *A Christmas Carol* in type than to some of his more outstanding achievements like *Great Expectations*. It is a fable drawn in very broad strokes-peopled with generally symbolic figures. The good characters are drawn thinly; the villains (Sikes, Fagin and Monks) are sketched in the blackest possible manner. Fagin is comical and somewhat sympathetic at times, compared to Sikes, but he is a caricature. The entire book has the enduring quality of a nightmare, interrupted briefly for the most transparent threads of sentimentality and **satire**. It is not a great novel, but it has great emotional appeal and an exciting story.

No greater testimony to Dickens' lasting power can be had than the fact that *Oliver Twist*, the product of an apprentice writer, has remained one of his most popular novels. So much so that it has been made into an excellent movie under the direction of David Lean, who also produced *Great Expectations*, and has appeared as a musical called Oliver in the 1965 season on Broadway.

BRIEF SUMMARY OF THE PLOT

A child, named Oliver Twist by the parish beadle, Mr. Bumble, was born to an unknown young woman in the parish workhouse. Sent until he was nine to a parish farm, he was then returned to the workhouse and set to work picking oakum. But after a short while, because he had asked for more food, a notice was posted offering five pounds to anyone who would take him as an apprentice. After nearly being apprenticed as a chimney sweep, he became the apprentice of Mr. Sowerberry, the local undertaker.

At Mr. Sowerberry's establishment Oliver was put to work as a "mute," dressed in black, to walk behind the hearse at funerals. And although he was treated by Mr. Sowerberry, he was mistreated by Mrs. Sowerberry; Charlotte, a slatternly servant girl; and Noah Claypole, a brutal charity boy also in Mr. Sowerberry's employ. As a result, one morning Oliver decided to run away. After seven days of walking, he arrived on the outskirts of London where he was greeted by a strangely dressed boy who called himself the Artful Dodger. Oliver was then taken by the Dodger to the den of Fagin, a master criminal.

At first Oliver did not realize that he had fallen in with thieves, but a few days later he watched the Dodgeo and Charley Bates pick an old gentleman's pocket, and he realized the truth. Running away at the cry of "thief," Oliver was mistakenly seized but was saved from jail by the intervention of the old gentleman, Mr. Brownlow, and the bookseller. He was then taken to Mr. Brownlow's home where he recovered from a serious fever, only to be kidnapped by Nancy and Bill Sikes, two of Fagin's accomplices, as he ran his first errand for Mr. Brownlow. Back in Fagin's clutches, Oliver was soon forced to participate in a burglary with Sikes and Toby Crackit, during which Oliver was shot and left by the two as they fled. However, Oliver recovered under the tender care of Mrs. Maylie, and her ward, Rose, who lived in the house which Sikes and Toby had attempted to rob.

Meanwhile back at the workhouse Mr. Bumble had married Mrs. Corney, the matron, who was now in possession of a locket and a ring which belonged to Oliver's mother. And through the intervention of Fagin, they were contacted by Monks (Edward Leeford), Oliver's half-brother, who bought and disposed of the jewelry. Monks had a pact with Fagin to make Oliver a criminal so that Oliver would be disinherited according to the terms of their father's will, a will which Monks' mother had destroyed.

After Oliver grew better, and Rose (who was also seriously ill for a time) recovered, they made attempts to find Mr. Brownlow but he had moved. Sikes, meanwhile, recovered under the care of Nancy, and was visited by Fagin who was anxious to have him return to work. Monks, still eager to have Oliver involved in criminal activities, plotted with Fagin to have him kidnapped again, but the plan was overheard by Nancy who had once before protected Oliver from the gang. This time she reported what she knew to Rose, who in turn informed Mr. Brownlow, recently returned from a trip to the West Indies. At a second meeting with Nancy, Mr. Brownlow recognized Monks from Nancy's description as the son of an old friend who had died.

A trap was laid and Monks was quickly ensnared. Although he attempted to deny his plot against Oliver, Mr. and Mrs. Bumble were forced to act as witnesses against him, and Monks was made to admit everything. Meanwhile Sikes, angry when he discovered what Nancy had done (Fagin had had her followed), killed Nancy, and the police put out a dragnet for the gang. Fagin and Noah were caught, and Fagin was sentenced to hang for his activities. Sikes was later trapped, hiding in a warehouse with Toby Crackit and Tom Pinch, fellow burglars, but accidentally hanged himself when he attempted to escape. Thus all the various strands of the plot were revealed. Rose, in reality Oliver's aunt, married Harry Maylie, Mrs. Maylie's nephew. Mr. Brownlow adopted Oliver, and went to live in the country, and Oliver's other benefactors came to the country to live nearby. Fagin was hanged and most of his gang imprisoned. Only Monks was allowed to escape. With the money Oliver gave him, he fled to America where he soon resumed a life of crime and spent the remainder of his life in prison.

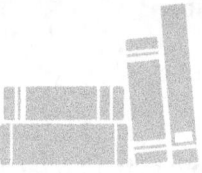

OLIVER TWIST

TEXTUAL ANALYSIS

CHAPTERS 1 - 15

CHAPTER ONE

Somewhere in a purposely unnamed town on an unstated day, a child was born to an unknown woman in the local workhouse. Attended by the parish surgeon and a beer-drinking midwife, she bore a sickly male child whose life hung in the balance. Asking to see the child, the frail young mother who had been found wandering the parish streets, had only time to kiss her child before she died. The child, Oliver, cried lustily, unaware of the hardships life was to hold for him.

Comment

Not only does **Chapter One** introduce the novel's major character, but admittedly withholds information concerning his parentage. Thus, the reader's attention will be held both by the surprising twists and turns of the plot, and by the mystery thus created.

CHAPTER TWO

Since the parish workhouse had no facilities for his care, Oliver was "farmed out" to a branch workhouse some three miles away where "juvenile offenders" "against the poor laws" were cared for. Here he was placed in the care of Mrs. Mann, whose neglect and whose thefts from the small sums, allotted for the care and feeding of her charges, had already resulted in the death of many of them.

Here, Oliver Twist, as he had been named by Mr. Bumble, the parish beadle, who named the orphans alphabetically, survived to his ninth birthday when Mr. Bumble returned to take him back to the workhouse in which he had been born. There the frightened Oliver was led before "eight or ten fat gentlemen" who made up the parish poor board, and was informed that hereafter he was to be allowed the privilege of picking oakum as a means of earning his keep.

Fed only a thin gruel as a matter of board policy to discourage pauperism, Oliver was a short while later chosen by the boys to ask for more to eat. Mr. Limbkins, the master, horrified, quickly reported Oliver to Mr. Bumble with the result that Oliver was instantly confined and the next morning a bill was posted offering five pounds to anyone who would relieve the parish of responsibility for him.

Comment

Not only is Dickens satirizing the Poor Law of 1834, but that form of charity which seeks to eliminate poverty by starving the poor.

It is also fitting that the representative of that kind of thinking should be Mr. Bumble, the parish beadle (a minor official who acts as overseer of the poor) - his name describes both the man and the thinking. He represents authority without dignity.

Examples of Dickens' ironic treatment of institutions and people who are objects of **satire** throughout the novel are seen in these early chapters. In **Chapter Two** he describes the callous members of the poor board with savage humor: "They found out at once, what ordinary folks would never have discovered - the poor people like it (workhouse). It was a regular place of public entertainment for the poorer classes.... They established the rule, that all poor people should have the alternative (for they would compel nobody, not they), of being starved by a gradual process in the house, or by a quick one out of it."

CHAPTER THREE

For a week Oliver remained in the solitary confinement of a darkened room for his disrespectfulness, and every other day was publicly flogged in the dining hall as a warning to those who might repeat his mistake. At the end of the week, however, Mr. Gamfield, a chimney sweep, chanced to read the bill offering the reward of five pounds and offered to take Oliver as his apprentice. The board, frightened at the possibility of bad publicity because Mr. Gamfield had already lost the lives of several of his previous apprentices, at first refused. But after reconsidering Mr. Gamfield's willingness to accept three pounds ten shillings instead of the five, the board quickly approved. Oliver was then released from his confinement by Mr. Bumble, given a clean shirt and a holiday allowance of food, and informed of his good fortune.

Later, brought before a local judge for approval of the apprenticeship, the frightened and trembling Oliver was questioned by the magistrate. Fortunately for Oliver, the nearsighted judge's search for his ink bottle caused him to look into Oliver's fear-stricken face. Touched, the magistrate, despite Mr. Bumble's protest, refused to sign the articles, and Oliver was returned to the workhouse where the bill offering five pounds to anyone who would take him was again quickly posted.

Comment

Chapter Three expands the criticism of the Poor Laws begun in **Chapter Two**, and prepares the way for eventful changes in Oliver's immediate future.

CHAPTER FOUR

After several inquiries in an attempt to place Oliver had failed, Mr. Bumble accidentally discovered in Mr. Sowerberry, the local undertaker, a person willing to take him as an apprentice. Having come to the workhouse on a matter related to the deaths of two women inmates on the previous evening, Mr. Sowerberry was overjoyed at the prospect of the five pound bonus. Accordingly, arrangements with the board were hurriedly made and Oliver was made ready for the transfer. Even Mr. Bumble was moved by Oliver's tears of fright and horror at leaving the only home he had ever known for an uncertain and probably unpleasant future.

Upon his arrival at Mr. Sowerberry's establishment, Oliver was immediately placed in the care of Mr. Sowerberry's unattractive and shrewish wife who transferred that care to Charlotte, a shabbily dressed servant girl. He was then given some scraps of meat usually reserved for the family dog, and assigned a bed under a counter in the coffin display room.

> Comment

Death, used as a symbolic device, helps to unify and intensify the allegorical struggle between good and evil which is at the novel's core. Not only had death been introduced several times in previous chapters (Oliver's mother, the workhouse inmates, and the chimney sweep apprentice of Mr. Gamfield), but it will be introduced for the same purpose many times throughout the story.

CHAPTER FIVE

Alone in a strange place Oliver spent an uncomfortable night and was awakened in the morning by the sound of someone kicking violently at the front door. Upon unfastening and opening the front door, he found himself confronted by the unfriendly sight of Noah Claypole, a charity boy also in the employ of Mr. Sowerberry. Following a kick from the large-headed, small-eyed Noah, Oliver was soon set to the task of taking down the heavy window shutters, and managed unfortunately to break a small pane in the process. And later, he was assigned to a corner at breakfast with some bits of stale bread while the loutish Noah dined on bacon which Charlotte had saved from the master's breakfast.

It was about a month later that Mr. Sowerberry decided to take the by now sad-expressioned Oliver along with him on his rounds in order to train him as a "mute" at funerals. Shortly thereafter Mr. Bumble provided a suitable opportunity, when Oliver and Mr. Sowerberry visited a filthy slum home to measure a young woman for a coffin. The next day they returned bringing a cheap coffin, no larger than necessary, and buried the young woman in a pauper's grave in a brief irreverent service, delayed by the late arrival of the clergyman.

Comment

Again Dickens takes the occasion to illustrate the plight of the poor. Oliver's role of "mute," or professional mourner, will be one of the many strange adventures which befall him in the course of the somewhat rambling novel.

CHAPTER SIX

Finally formally apprenticed, after having passed his "month's trial" with the funeral director, Oliver was now suitably dressed for his role as "mute." And for many months he bore the unpleasant occupation, as well as the ill-treatment of the brutal Noah, Charlotte, and Mrs. Sowerberry, who were either jealous or annoyed because of his new importance to Mr. Sowerberry. However, finally goaded too far by Noah's taunts about his mother, Oliver knocked the larger boy down. The cowardly Noah ran screaming for help to Mrs. Sowerberry and Charlotte, and all of them joined in beating the helpless Oliver. After they had locked him in the dark coal cellar beneath the shop, Noah ran at full speed to Mr. Bumble to report Oliver's murderous attack.

Comment

Although Oliver is alone and nearly helpless, his courage does not fail him. The attack upon him by the three adults represents still another side of Dickens' criticism of Victorian society, for in this society not only do adults suffer from brutal and inhumane treatment, but children as well.

CHAPTER SEVEN

After receiving Noah's report that Oliver had "turned vicious" and "tried to murder" him, Mr. Bumble hurried to the undertakers with Noah. Here he heard Oliver still kicking violently against the inside of the cellar door. Attempting then to intimidate Oliver by his presence and by threats, Mr. Bumble succeeded only in further enraging the angry Oliver. Finally, Mr. Sowerberry returned and was told the exaggerated tale of Oliver's rebellion, and he opened the door and dragged Oliver out of the cellar. Although Mr. Sowerberry did not believe much of what he had been told, he was forced to punish Oliver severely because at that moment Mrs. Sowerberry burst into tears. Mr. Sowerberry, more afraid of his wife's displeasure than fond of Oliver, gave Oliver a sound beating and shut him up in the back kitchen, though not without first giving him a slice of bread.

For a long time Oliver crouched alone crying. Finally tying a few belongings in a handkerchief, he waited until the first light of morning and crept out of the house. Finding a road that he remembered, he set out toward the workhouse farm where he had spent his childhood. Here he found little Dick, a former friend and inmate who had often shared his hardships. After Oliver had informed Dick of his plan to run away and seek his fortune, Dick told Oliver that he was dying and flung his arms around Oliver's neck, blessing him. Promising that he would return, Oliver proceeded on his journey bearing "the first blessing ever invoked upon him."

Comment

Little Dick, like many of Dickens' children and women, is more symbolic than a flesh-and-blood person. It was Dickens' long held belief that his portrayal of such angelic and pathetic characters might awaken the Victorian conscience. Dickens firmly believed that the lot of the lower classes could best be improved by a change in the hearts of men. That Dickens often reduced his moralizing to the level of exaggerated sentimentality and bathos cannot be denied. However, his own personal compassion was genuine and won the hearts of the Victorian reading public.

CHAPTER EIGHT

Walking steadily until noon, Oliver sat down to rest on a road marker seventy miles from London, and believing London a good place to hide, he soon set out again. The first day he covered twenty miles, "begging at cottage doors for a crust of bread" until cold and hungry he spent the night in a haystack. The next morning he set out again, but on this day he covered only twelve miles, and was forced to spend his sole coin for a small loaf of bread. With little success, he begged from coach passengers, farmers, and villagers. And after seven days with the kindness of a turnpipe-man who fed him, he arrived cold, hungry, and exhausted in the little town of Barnet where every other building seemed to be a tavern. As he crouched, shivering on a doorstep, he was accosted by a strangely dressed, bowlegged boy about his own age. "What's the row?" the boy wanted to know. Not only was the boy dressed strangely, but he spoke even more strangely. Finally, however, after Oliver had explained that he was cold and hungry, the young man bought him some bread and ham for supper and offered to find him a place in London with a "spectable old genllman" who would provide lodging for nothing.

Later that evening Jack Dawkins, or the Artful Dodger as he preferred to be called, led Oliver by a twisting route through filthy back alleys and streets of the Saffron Hill slum district of London. Here at the bottom of the hill, after calling "plummy and slam" at a disreputable looking house, they were admitted and led up a dirty, broken staircase into a very dirty room containing four or five boys and a "villainous looking," "old shriveled Jew" called Fagin. Introduced by the Dodger, Oliver shook hands with Fagin, who grinned evilly and bowed to him. And after the boys had laughed loudly at Oliver's wonderment over the great number of handkerchiefs which seemed to be hung about the room, he was given some sausages for dinner and put to bed on some old sacks where he soon feel asleep.

Comment

As a young reporter, Dickens had wandered extensively throughout London and its suburbs. And as a result, nearly all of his books contain faithful descriptions of persons and places which he had actually seen in his travels. In addition, the description of the Saffron Hill slum reveals Dickens' belief that the visible signs of decay evident in Victorian England were signs of a much greater moral decay which lay beneath the surface.

The Artful Dodger is one of Dickens' memorable fictional portraits. He is "tagged" (in typical Dickensian fashion) with a unique colloquial speech, a distinctive physical description, and odd gestures (a sudden twitch of the head to keep his hat from falling off). His description in this chapter is typical of Dickens' skillful use of minute details.

CHAPTER NINE

Late the next morning when Oliver awoke, he found himself alone with the old Hew Fagin, who was whistling to himself as he cooked coffee in an old saucepan. As he watched, the old man, who was unaware that Oliver was awake, pulled a small box out of a trap door in the floor from which he withdrew a quantity of glittering jewels. Suddenly the old man discovered Oliver watching, slammed the box closed and picked up a bread knife. Then pretending that he had picked up the knife as a joke, he told Oliver that the jewels were his "little property" "to live upon in my old age."

Shortly thereafter the Dodger returned, accompanied by a young man whom he introduced to Oliver as Charley Bates, and the four sat down to breakfast. During breakfast the boys reported to Fagin and showed him two pocketbooks and four handkerchiefs which Oliver assumed they had made. After breakfast the two boys took turns playing a game which consisted of picking each other's pockets. Interrupted in their game by the arrival of Bet and Nancy, two young ladies whom Oliver thought "very nice indeed," Charley and the Dodger and the two young ladies left gaily, having apparently received some money from Fagin to spend.

Oliver, now alone with Fagin, was further instructed in the pickpocket game and advised that he would do well to take Charley and the Dodger as his "models" for conduct. Finally Fagin gave him a shilling and put him to work removing marks out of the many handkerchiefs in the room.

Comment

Oliver's innocence is, of course, his greatest enemy. Having no experience of the world he is unable to realize that he has fallen in with thieves. All his life Dickens was interested in crime and criminals and the description of their activities reveals still another facet of his accurate portrayal of Victorian society. **Chapters Eight** and **Nine** introduce the reader to one of the most colorful, famous villains in all of English Literature. He symbolizes the evil power of the London underworld, guarding his treasure like a dragon in a fairy tale. His dominant physical feature is "matted red hair." When Oliver is taken in, Fagin's den is both the dungeon and a place of refuge. At times it is even cheerful. Cut off from true moral values, however, it is doomed to collapse, but not before Fagin and his gang have sacrificed the lives and fortunes of many innocent victims.

CHAPTER TEN

For many days Oliver continued in his occupation of picking marks out of handkerchiefs, and sometimes took part in the pickpocket game. At length, it was decided that he might go out in the care of Charley and the Dodger. At first believing that Charley and the Dodger intended to deceive Fagin by not going to work, Oliver was both surprised and horrified when the Dodger plunged his hand into the pocket of an old gentleman who was looking over some books at an outdoor bookstall. Frightened and confused by this turn of events, Oliver began to run just as the old gentleman, aware that his handkerchief was missing, loudly shouted "stop thief." The cry was taken up by a hundred voices and in that instant Oliver found himself pursued by an angry horde which by now included his former friends Charley and the Dodger. Cornered at last, Oliver was knocked down by a large fat man, and lay cut and bleeding on the dusty pavement. Dragged to his feet, he was saved from further punishment at the hands of the crowd by the timely arrival of the old gentleman and a police officer who seized him by the collar. Firmly held in the officer's grasp, Oliver attempted to no avail to declare his innocence and was dragged along by his collar to the magistrate, followed by a curious and noisy crowd.

Comment

Now aware in this crucial chapter of the real character of his friends, Oliver will be befriended by the old gentleman, Mr. Brownlow, whose friendship will play a large part later in unraveling the mystery of Oliver's birth.

CHAPTER ELEVEN

Dragged to jail, Oliver was locked in a small, dark, dirty cell to await the presence of Mr. Fang, the magistrate. Even though Mr. Brownlow did not wish to press charges because he was uncertain of Oliver's guilt, he was told that he must. Presently Mr. Fang was ready and Oliver was led into his imposing presence. Angrily Mr. Fang forced Mr. Brownlow to be sworn as a witness against Oliver despite Mr. Brownlow's protests. Oliver, too frightened to speak in his own defense, fainted, whereupon Mr. Fang, convinced that Oliver was faking, sentenced him to three months in prison. However, at that moment the bookstall keeper whose book Mr. Brownlow had accidentally kept during the chase, arrived to testify that Oliver was innocent. Angrily Mr. Fang had them all removed from the office. Outside, the kindly Mr. Brownlow called a coach and with the help of the bookseller lifted Oliver inside and took him home.

> Comment

Mr. Brownlow's recognition of something familiar in Oliver's face is a **foreshadowing** of events to come. Mr. Fang, the police magistrate, is, of course, aptly described by his name. He is a portrait from real life Dickens had witnessed a trial similar to the one he describes in this chapter.

CHAPTER TWELVE

For many days Oliver remained unconscious and when he finally awoke thin and pale, he wanted to know where he was. He was answered almost immediately by Mrs. Bedwin, Mr. Brownlow's housekeeper. Calmed by Mrs. Bedwin, Oliver lay back on the bed; she looked at him in the same strange manner as had Mr. Brownlow at the police station. Some days later, his condition improved, Oliver found his attention drawn to a portrait of a young woman hanging on a wall. Mrs. Bedwin and Mr. Brownlow did not fail to note the similarity of Oliver's features to those of the young woman in the portrait. In fact, Mr. Brownlow's, exclamation to that effect caused Oliver to faint.

Meanwhile, having escaped in the confusion following Oliver's capture, the Artful Dodger and Charley Bates returned to Fagin's lair, fearful of how he would react to their failure to return with Oliver.

> Comment

Again Dickens employs the device of fore-shadowing. The young woman in the portrait will later prove to be Oliver's mother. This chapter also introduces a device familiar not only in the nineteenth-century novel, but in melodrama. In this case, Oliver's meeting with Mr. Brownlow and his experience with the portrait are the first of many coincidences by which the plot is advanced.

CHAPTER THIRTEEN

Immediately aware that Oliver was missing, Fagin seized the Dodger by the collar and demanded to know where he was. Told that Oliver was in jail, the angry Fagin struggled with the Dodger and threw a beer pot at him. However, at this point, the struggle was interrupted by the arrival of Bill Sikes, a bulky scowling man accompanied by a dirty-white shaggy dog. Sikes, splashed by the beer, demanded to know who threw the beer pot at him, but was calmed by Fagin, who supplied him with two or three glasses of liquor. In the discussion which followed, Fagin related his fear that Oliver might tell the police about them, and Sikes, aware that Oliver had obviously not yet talked, concluded that they must get hold of Oliver before he could.

Interrupted at this point by the arrival of Bet and Nancy, they hit upon the plan of sending Nancy, who was not known to the police in this particular district, to find out what had happened to Oliver. Pretending to be Oliver's sister, she was told by the police that Oliver had been taken ill following his acquittal and had been taken home by the "old gentleman" who lived somewhere in Pentonville. Having thus gathered the required information, Nancy hurried back to Bill Sikes and Fagin at the latter's place. No sooner had Bill Sikes heard this information than he left with his dog, and Fagin instructed Nancy and Charley to go out and seek further information concerning Oliver's whereabouts. A short while later, interrupted by the Artful Dodger, Fagin revealed that Oliver was to be kidnapped before he could "blab us among his new friends."

Comment

The vicious Bill Sikes, accompanied by his equally vicious dog, Bull's-Eye, is the arch-villain of the novel. Although Fagin is also a villain, his portrayal is not unrelieved by humor, nor is he entirely unmotivated. Sikes, on the other hand, represents absolute evil. He steals, destroys, and murders as much for pleasure as for profit. He lives and will die by violence.

CHAPTER FOURTEEN

Oliver soon recovered from the fainting fit into which Mr. Brownlow's exclamation had thrown him. But the subject of his resemblance to the portrait was now avoided, and the portrait was itself removed. Under Mrs. Bedwin's tender care, Oliver soon recovered fully, and the days which followed were happy ones. Oliver was supplied with the first new suit of clothes that he had ever owned.

About a week later, Oliver was called by Mr. Brownlow to his study, a pleasant room lined with books. Here Mr. Brownlow offered to begin Oliver's education, and questioned Oliver about his past life. But as Oliver began to relate how he had been brought up at the farm, and carried to the workhouse by Mr. Bumble, they were interrupted by the arrival of Mr. Grimwig, a friend of Mr. Brownlow. A few moments later they were again interrupted by Mrs. Bedwin who brought a small parcel of books which had just been delivered by a boy from the same bookstall where Oliver and Mr. Brownlow had first met. Because the boy had left without payment and because there were some books to be returned, the honest Mr. Brownlow was disturbed. And Oliver, feeling much indebted to Mr. Brownlow, offered to attend to the matter for him. Given a five-pound note and a small parcel of books, Oliver then hurried after the boy.

After Oliver had left, Mr. Brownlow announced to the skeptical Mr. Grimwig that Oliver would return "in twenty minutes, at the longest," a prediction which the pessimistic Mr. Grimwig doubted. Not that Mr. Grimwig was a malevolent man, but he believed that Oliver, a workhouse orphan, would be too greatly tempted by the new suit of clothes, the five-pound note, and a parcel of valuable books. Although the two old gentlemen sat in silence, the watch between them until it was dark, Oliver did not return.

Comment

Mr. Grimwig is as his name suggests, a grim, pessimistic man whose head is rarely penetrated by optimistic beliefs. Oliver's errand corresponds roughly to the quest upon which a young knight was sent to prove himself in medieval tales. Oliver would have proven himself well if left to his own devices, but the reader has already had warning that trouble is brewing. Suspense mounts as the two gentlemen watch the clock.

CHAPTER FIFTEEN

In a dirty public house in Saffron Hill, Bill Sikes sat drinking, accompanied by his red-eyed quarrelsome dog. Angry, disturbed, and partly drunk, Sikes suddenly kicked at the dog who retaliated by sinking his teeth into Sikes boot. A few moments later the by now violent struggle between man and dog was interrupted by Fagin who had come to pay Sikes his share of the proceeds for a recent robbery. As the two drank, they were joined by a younger edition of Fagin, Barney, a young Jew who reported that Nancy was eating in the bar. Ushered in, Nancy, still in the costume she used at the police station, reported new information as to Oliver's whereabouts. A few moments later, Nancy, accompanied by Bill Sikes left the tavern.

Meanwhile Oliver, a short distance away, was on his way to the bookstall. As he walked, he was suddenly accosted by a young woman who announced that he was her "dear brother" and he was seized by her. As Oliver attempted to explain to passersby that he was not her brother, Bill Sikes, pretending to be a passersby rushed to Nancy' aid, tore away the books Oliver was carrying and grasped him firmly by the collar. Then commanding the growling Bull's-Eye to guard Oliver, marched the overpowered frightened Oliver away to encouraging cries of the deluded spectators.

Back at Mr. Brownlow's, Mrs. Bedwin and the two old gentlemen still waited patiently.

Comment

Again Dickens draws together diverse plot elements. Matters hinted at in **Chapter Thirteen** are now an actuality. The interruption afforded by **Chapters Fourteen** and **Fifteen** is an important device Dickens used to create suspense in the various installments of a serial story.

The name of the Saffron Hill Public House, the Three Cripples, describes very well the three who meet there.

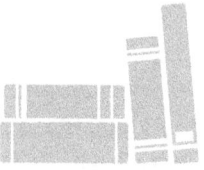

OLIVER TWIST

TEXTUAL ANALYSIS

CHAPTERS 16 - 28

CHAPTER SIXTEEN

Dragged through narrow streets, backyards, and alleys by Sikes and Nancy, Oliver soon found himself before the door of a boarded up and seemingly uninhabited shop. At a signal from Nancy, the door was opened and the terrified Oliver was dragged into a dark passageway where a light was finally lit. Oliver found himself confronted by Charley Bates, the Artful Dodger, and Fagin.

Soon stripped of his new clothes, the five pounds, and the packet of books he had been carrying, Oliver found himself again clothed in his old rags which Fagin had bought from the old clothes dealer to whom they had been sold. Angry and afraid at the same time, Oliver protested that the books and the money were the property of his benefactor, Mr. Brownlow. And finally more afraid that Mr. Brownlow would think him a thief than of Fagin and Sikes, Oliver made a sudden dash to escape. Fortunately Nancy saved him from pursuit by Bill Sikes' dangerous dog by slamming shut the door to the room behind the fleeing Oliver. But the pursuit was quickly taken up by Fagin and the two boys who dragged the struggling Oliver back into the room. Then struck across the shoulders by the angry Fagin, who wielded a jagged and knotted club, Oliver was again saved by the intervention of Nancy who insisted violently that they had already done enough to hurt him. Not even the threats of the angry Sikes and Fagin persuaded the by now frightened and hysterical Nancy to give up her protection of Oliver, until finally, seized by Sikes, the frenzied girl fainted. At this Oliver was led into an old kitchen in which there were three beds, and locked up for the night. Through the door he heard the arrival of Miss Betsy, who helped to revive the stricken Nancy.

Comment

A careful reading of **Chapter Thirteen** makes Nancy's protection of Oliver in this chapter more understandable. Although she had led a life of vice and crime, and although she helped in the kidnapping of Oliver, she did these things reluctantly. Dickens presents Nancy as a tragic victim of circumstance. Unlike Bill Sikes, who is intrinsically evil, Nancy is a by-product of a cruel social system. Though living in a thieves' world, she is still capable of some measure of compassion, courage, and virtue. The scene in this chapter foreshadows the future aid she will give to Oliver.

CHAPTER SEVENTEEN

Back at the workhouse where Oliver had been born, Mr. Bumble emerged from the workhouse gate, and walked quickly through town until he arrived at the parochial farm where Mrs. Mann tended the town's infant paupers. Here he was admitted respectfully by the fawning Mrs. Mann. After he announced pompously that he was going to London on business, he gave Mrs. Mann the money with which she was to operate the farm and care for the foundlings there for the next month. Then after she gave Mr. Bumble a receipt, Mrs. Mann brought in the by now very ill Little Dick, who asked if someone would write a letter in which he could leave his "dear love to poor Oliver Twist." Thereupon Mrs. Mann and Mr. Bumble started in mixed astonishment and anger that any charge of the town should dare to want for anything. Finally Mr. Bumble demanded that the "hardened little wretch" be removed from his sight.

Later that evening at an inn where his coach had stopped for the night, Mr. Bumble happened to see an advertisement in a newspaper offering "five guineas reward" to anyone who could supply information past or present about Oliver Twist. Excited by the prospect of reward, Mr. Bumble left hurriedly for Pentonville, and a short while later was at Mr. Brownlow's door. Here, after being admitted, he was greeted by Mrs. Bedwin whose anxiety caused her to burst into tears, and Mr. Bumble was led upstairs to Mr. Brownlow's study where Mr. Brownlow and Mr. Grimwig awaited. After greetings had been exchanged, Mr. Bumble informed Mr. Brownlow of Oliver's low, "treacherous" past. Saddened by the information, Mr. Brownlow declared "that boy, Oliver, is an imposter" and forbade Mrs. Bedwin to mention his name again. Although Mr. Grimwig was delighted to have his previous opinion of Oliver confirmed, Mrs. Bedwin still steadfastly refused to believe Mr. Bumble's account.

Comment

Since parish children received no education, Little Dick could not write, and was thus forced to ask someone to write the letter to Oliver for him. Mr. Bumble's chance reading of Mr. Brownlow's advertisement is another use by Dickens of the familiar device of coincidence, a technique used to unify diverse plot elements.

CHAPTER EIGHTEEN

About noon the next day after the Dodger and Charley Bates had left, Fagin lectured Oliver on ingratitude. He reminded Oliver that he had taken him in when he was in difficulty, and related to Oliver a similar story of another boy who had finally been hanged at Old Bailey, the famous London prison. Following this information, Fagin's threats were less veiled and he concluded by reminding Oliver that if Oliver attempted to inform the police, they would probably conclude that Oliver was a guilty as the rest. Satisfied at last that Oliver understood, Fagin then locked him up in the kitchen for a week, after which he was allowed to wander about the dark, dirty, moldering old house.

One evening Oliver engaged in a rather lengthy and generally good natured conversation with the Dodger and Charley in which they attempted to persuade Oliver to join the gang. And though Oliver did not wish to become a criminal, he found the company of the Dodger and Charley pleasant. A few days later, Fagin arrived, accompanied by Miss Betsy and a young man named Tom Chitling, who had recently been released from jail. All then sat around the fire and told happy tales about the joys of their trade. Thus many pleasant evenings were passed until Fagin believed that he had Oliver firmly "in his toils."

Comment

Unable to break Oliver's will by threat and confinement, Fagin now cleverly resorted to following such punishment with kindness, hoping that Oliver's enjoyment of such kindness would encourage him to volunteer to join the group. He, of course, is not aware that Oliver is made of sterner stuff, for Oliver will never voluntarily submit to a life of evil. Once aspect of Oliver's tragedy is that Fagin's household represents two conflicting and diametrically opposed things to the boy. At the same time that it represents evil, it is a tragic **parody** of normal home life. In this, the only "home" that Oliver has ever known, there is sometimes a warmth (of sorts) to which Oliver responds. Fagin dances, the group tells tales by the fireside, etc. But the outer picture belies the inner decay. Oliver can never find in Fagin's world the sense of identity and security he seeks.

CHAPTER NINETEEN

Finally, one damp and windy night, Fagin dressed warmly and left his den, carefully chaining the door behind him. After glancing suspiciously around, he hurried through the muddy streets and alleys to a house in Bethnal Green. Here he was admitted to the house occupied by Bill Sikes and Nancy. And there over a glass of brandy from which Fagin and Sikes drank in turn, they discussed plans for the robbery of a house in Chertsey. An accomplice of Sikes, Toby Crackit, had hung around the house for a week; he had been unable to strike up an acquaintance with any of the servants. Thus, discouraged, Sikes was tempted to give up the job, but decided that it could still be done if he had the assistance of a small boy who could be pushed in through a small window.

At this point, Fagin reminded Sikes that Oliver might become more involved in their criminal web if he were used in the robbery at hand. Accordingly, it was agreed that the robbery would take place the next night since there would be no moon, and Oliver would be brought beforehand to Sikes' room by Nancy. These matters settled, Fagin left for his own lair where he gazed upon the innocently sleeping Oliver and decided to delay telling Oliver about their decision until tomorrow.

Comment

Although Fagin obviously wishes to involve Oliver in the gang's criminal activities so he cannot "peach" or talk, he has another reason, which will be revealed later in the novel with the introduction of Monks (**Chapter Twenty-Six**), Oliver's half-brother. **Chapter Nineteen** marked the end of the ninth installment (December, 1837) of *Oliver Twist*. Dickens left Oliver on the brink of a new, precarious adventure; and undoubtedly he left his readers breathless for the next serial segment.

CHAPTER TWENTY

The following morning when Oliver awoke, he was surprised to find alongside his bed a new pair of shoes with thick soles. Believing at first that he might be released, he soon discovered at breakfast that he was to be taken to Bill Sikes that evening. And when he asked why he was to be sent, he was told that he would have to "wait till Bill tells you." Then with apparent kindness Fagin supplied Oliver with a candle and a book to read until it was time to go. At first puzzled, the horrified Oliver soon discovered that the book was "a History of the lives and trials of great criminals" and its pages "soiled and thumbed with use." Fearfully Oliver closed the book and "prayed to heaven to spare him from such deeds." Gradually he grew calm and remained alone "in the midst of wickedness and guilt" with his head buried in his hands.

From this position he was later aroused by Nancy, who begged God's forgiveness, and told Oliver that she had come to bring him to Sikes. Not only was Oliver aware that Nancy was sorry for him, but that she might help him to escape. However, Nancy, sensing Oliver's understanding, told him that now was not the time. Promising to help Oliver as she had in the past, she showed him some livid bruises on her arms and neck and reminded him that every word from him "is a blow for me." She pointed out also that if she had not come "to fetch" Oliver, those who would have come would have been rougher. At this the two clutched each other by the hand, and went shrouded in darkness to a cab which was waiting outside, where without direction, the driver "lashed the horse with full speed" to Sikes' house.

At the house, Sikes lectured his young "pupil." He showed Oliver a pistol which he then loaded and held to Oliver's head. Sikes threatened that if Oliver ever decided to cross him, he would kill him. These pleasantries completed, the table was set and Sikes, Nancy and Oliver sat down to a supper of "porter (a kind of beer) and sheeps' heads." After dinner, Sikes instructed Nancy to call him at five, and he and Oliver stretched out on a mattress upon the floor to sleep. When Oliver awoke, it was not yet quite daylight, but Sikes was already awake and thrusting various articles, including his pistol, into the pocket of his greatcoat (overcoat). After a hasty breakfast, prepared by Nancy, Sikes and Oliver left the house.

Comment

At this point, although Nancy wishes to help Oliver, she is still too afraid of the gang, and her loyalty to Sikes is far too strong. Note too how Dickens again maintains suspense by ending the chapter at a high point.

CHAPTER TWENTY-ONE

It was a cheerless morning, rainy and windy, as Oliver and Sikes made their way toward London. Through a maze of streets, alleys, and marketplaces, Sikes dragged Oliver until they had passed through the heart of the city where, near Kensington, they came upon an empty cart. Here Sikes, convincing the driver that he and Oliver were father and son, secured a ride for them. At a public house called the Coach and Horses, Oliver and Sikes got out and the driver continued on his way. After hiding in some fields nearby, the returned and entered the public house where they had some dinner and Sikes engaged a man in conversation. Sometime after dark, since they had traveled throughout the better part of a day, Oliver and Sikes got into the wagon of the man for whom Sikes had bought drinks, and they set out again. Hours later in the evening they came to Shepperton where Oliver and Sikes dismounted. Seeing they were somewhere near water, Oliver at first feared Sikes meant to murder him, but instead, they stopped before a house "ruinous and decayed." Here, Sikes opened a door at the side of the darkened and dilapidated house and they entered.

Comment

The journey through London and its suburbs reveals Dickens' great knowledge of the area. As a young reporter for the *Morning Chronicle*, he had traveled widely. Critics have often noted that Dickens reproduced the geography of London with almost minute faithfulness to all details. It has been noted that *Oliver Twist* could be used as an accurate map of the areas Dickens described in the 1830s.

Note too how Dickens uses atmosphere to reenforce the action in his story. For example, bad weather always indicates the coming of some evil event, and the desolate scenery provides an appropriate locale for it.

CHAPTER TWENTY-TWO

The house, however, was not unoccupied. Inside Oliver and Sikes were greeted by Toby Crackit, a dirty, red haired man, and Barney, the waiter from the Three Cripples. They drank to the success of "the crack," the robbery, which was planned for that evening, and discussed Oliver's possible future as a criminal (which Toby thought great because of Oliver's innocent appearing face). Later they all lay down to rest until it was time to leave.

At half-past one Oliver was awakened by Toby Crackit, who loudly announced the time, and preparations for the robbery were hurriedly completed. Toby thrust two pistols which had been prepared by Barney into his pockets, and attached to the inside skirts of his coat the other burglar tools which might be required in the robbery. Still somewhat sleepy from the long day and the wine which he had been made to drink, Oliver was pulled through the door of the house between the two robbers.

By now it was very dark, and although the rain had stopped, it was much foggier that it had been earlier. As a result the two robbers decided to go through the town instead of around it. By two o'clock after clearing the town, they stood before a wall which surrounded a house. Hoisted over the wall by Sikes, Oliver lay with the two robbers on the grass on the other side facing the house. Now, for the first time, the terrified Oliver realized that he was "to take part in robbery, if not murder." Held firmly by the angry Sikes, Oliver struggled and pleaded for mercy, and was only saved from Sikes' murderous rage by Toby who knocked Sikes' pistol away from Oliver's head because it would have made too much noise. Though still seething with anger, Sikes released Oliver and pried open a shutter which concealed a small latticed window about five and a half feet above the ground at the rear of the house. Believing Oliver now frightened enough to do as he was told, Sikes put Oliver through the open window, and instructed him to go along the hall inside and unfasten the street door. Oliver, almost fainting, dropped into the room as Sikes kept him covered with the pistol.

Once inside Oliver let his lantern fall and cried aloud, determined to awaken those in the house. Almost immediately a light appeared at the top of a stairway which outlined two half-dressed men. A shot was fired, followed by the discharge of Sikes' pistol behind Oliver in reply. Dragged by his collar, Oliver was then pulled back out of the room and wrapped in a shawl by Sikes who shouted to Toby "They've hit him. Quick! How the boy bleeds." The ringing of a loud bell, the noise of firearms and shouting men were the last sounds which Oliver heard before he lost consciousness.

Comment

Five chapters will intervene before the reader discovers how badly Oliver is hurt. Meanwhile Dickens turns to other strands of the complicated plot. Although the delay for modern readers is only a few chapters, those who read the original *Oliver Twist* as a serial had to wait two months for the next installment to discover Oliver's fate. Such treatment leaves the novel with a significant lack of overall unity and a certain episodic flavor.

Note the very typical Dickensian character name in this section - Toby Crackit, an appropriate name for a burglar.

CHAPTER TWENTY-THREE

On a bitterly cold, bleak night back at the workhouse where Oliver was born, Mrs. Corney, the matron, sat before the fire in her own room preparing a cup of tea. As she proceeded to make the tea, she was disturbed by a soft tap at the door to her room. Annoyed because she believed that one of the inmates was dying, Mrs. Corney was surprised to hear Mr. Bumble's voice in the hallway. And after being admitted, Mr. Bumble sat with Mrs. Corney over tea and discussed the ingratitude of the paupers in their care, with particular regard to the case of a pauper who had actually demanded of Mr. Grannet, the local overseer, enough to eat. Mr. Bumble, greedily eyed Mrs. Corney's possessions displayed about the room. And because he believed a small flirtation might not be rejected by her, he moved his chair closer to hers. Just as he placed his arm about her, and she announced that she was about to scream, they were interrupted by the knock at the door. The two leaped apart; as Mr. Bumble pretended clumsily to be dusting some wine bottles, Mrs. Corney demanded to know who was there. At this an aged female pauper stuck her head into the doorway and announced that Old Sally was "a-going fast."

Informed that Old Sally would not die without first speaking to her, the annoyed Mrs. Corney requested Mr. Bumble to wait and left the room. Mr. Bumble, left alone, proceeded to carefully inspect the contents of the room, especially a silver milk pot to see if it were "of genuine metal." And he finally settled himself comfortably before the fire where he seemed to be mentally engaged in taking an inventory of the furniture.

> Comment

Mr. Grannet, the overseer, is a man whose heart is made of granite. Old Sally, you will remember, was the old woman who had acted as midwife at Oliver's birth. Her re-introduction is a **foreshadowing** of events to come, for what she has to tell Mrs. Corney will be important to Oliver later in the story.

The conversation between Mrs. Corney and Mr. Bumble, of course, is another chapter in Dickens' continuing **satire** on the Poor Laws. Their idea of relief, and the idea apparently of those who administered the Poor Laws, was "to give the paupers exactly what they don't want, and then they get tired of coming."

CHAPTER TWENTY-FOUR

Mrs. Corney followed the aged, trembling old inmate to a bare attic room where Old Sally lay dying. Here she was greeted by the local druggist's apprentice who stood whittling a piece of wood by a fire in an attempt to warm the cold room. And as another old woman stood watching by the bed, Mrs. Corney listened as the apprentice repeated the information that Old Sally was near death. After determining that Old Sally was not yet dead, but only asleep she sat at the foot of the bed and waited impatiently. Finally as Mrs. Corney was about to leave, Old Sally awakened, drew Mrs. Corney close to the bed and demanded that the two other inmates in the room leave. When they had left, she told Mrs. Corney her story.

Long ago, she related, a young woman had given birth to a boy, then died in this very bed. After the girl had died, Old Sally had stolen something made of gold which the girl had worn about her neck. This unnamed article, which the young mother had asked Old Sally to keep for her child, Sally had kept for herself. And now, Old Sally, near death, wanted to return the article to the child whose name she remembered was Oliver. But before Mrs. Corney was able to discover what the mysterious gold object was, Old Sally rose on the bed, fell back and died. "Stone dead" said the old inmates admitted again to the room. To this, Mrs. Corney replied lying, "and nothing to tell, after all." Thereupon Mrs. Corney hurried from the room and left the old women to prepare Old Sally's body for burial.

Comment

It appears at first that Mrs. Corney has not secured the information she wanted from Old Sally. Actually she knows where to find the gold article because clutched in Old Sally's hand she found a pawn ticket. Moreover, the two old women who had been sent from the room had listened at the door and watched through the keyhole. Dickens, for purposes of suspense, often withholds such important information, only to spring it on the unwary reader as a surprise later in the story. Such a device belongs, many critics believe, more properly to melodrama than to the novel. But because Dickens was all his life interested in the theater, he employed many of the devices of that medium in his novels.

CHAPTER TWENTY-FIVE

While these events took place at the workhouse, Fagin sat in the old den from which Oliver had been removed, attempting to rouse a smoky fire. Behind him, the Dodger, Charley Bates, and Tom Chitling played Whist. As they played, the Dodger, a clay pipe between his teeth, won another point, and Tom complained that the "Dodger has such a run of luck that there's no standing again him." After the game, the three teased Tom because he was in love with Betsy until the angry Tom reminded Fagin that if he had talked during his recent jail term, Fagin and his friends might not now be so jolly. Tom's angry outburst was at that moment interrupted by the sound of the doorbell, and the Dodger went down to see who was there. Nervous at the information whispered to him by the Dodger, that Toby Crackit had arrived alone, Fagin ordered the boys out of the room. A few moments later, Toby, guided by the Dodger, entered the room, and Fagin waited anxiously while the haggard, unshaven, hungry man ate and drank. Finally when Toby had finished with his meal, he asked the surprised and shocked Fagin "How's Bill?" He was himself shocked and frightened to discover that Fagin had not heard from Sikes either. Informed by Toby that the robbery, completed three days earlier had failed, Fagin pulled a newspaper from his pocket which had already supplied him with that information. However, now confronted by Toby, who revealed that he and Sikes had left Oliver seriously wounded in a ditch, and had gone their separate ways, Fagin trembled, fearful of what this news might mean to them all. Finally, tearing his hair with a wild yell, he fled from the house.

Comment

Not only is Fagin afraid that Bill Sikes may have been caught, or that Oliver may tell what he knows about them all, but as we shall later discover, he is violently disturbed because Oliver is very valuable to him. Toby's information also reminds the reader that Oliver has been seriously wounded, and renews the reader's interest in that matter so abruptly suspended in **Chapter Twenty-two**.

CHAPTER TWENTY-SIX

Before Fagin reached the corner, he had in large part recovered himself. However, he did not slow down, but pressed on in the same disordered manner through byways and alleys until he finally emerged into the Saffron Hill district where the filthy shops seemed to specialize in the sale of secondhand silk handkerchiefs. Here in Fish Lane, which Fagin knew well, he inquired of a shopkeeper if Sikes was at the Three Cripples. But although he was told that Sikes was not there, Fagin decided to go alone. Three, with a sign to the barman, Fagin went upstairs to a room in which some kind of a party was being held. Finally making a sign to the chairman of the group, Fagin left the room and waited. Soon he was joined on the landing by the chairman who was also the landlord of the Three Cripples, and he asked again for Sikes. Although the landlord had not seen Sikes or Barney, he reassured Fagin that Barney must be all right or he would have heard. Unable to secure any information about Sikes or Barney, Fagin then inquired if "he" would be in tonight. But in response to the information that Mr. Monks would be in shortly, Fagin left a message that he (Monks) must come to see him the following night, and hurriedly left.

Outside Fagin hailed a horse-drawn cab and drove toward Sikes' place in Bethnal Green, walking the last quarter mile on foot. When he received no response to his knock, Fagin crept into the room where Nancy sat with her head sprawled on the table. Roused by the sound of Fagin's entry, Nancy listened to Fagin's recital of Toby's story and sank back on the table. Although Fagin attempted to get information about Sikes' possible whereabouts, he was unsuccessful. Nancy only hoped that Oliver was dead, for he would then be "better where he is than among us."

Angrily Fagin responded that Sikes had better report to him as soon as he returned because the "boy's worth hundreds of pounds to me." Almost instantly, he regretted his outburst and hoped that the listless girl had not paid any attention to his words. And after easing his mind that Nancy had not understood the meaning of his words, Fagin left Nancy asleep with her head again on the kitchen table.

Comment

Although Nancy pretends she has not understood Fagin, she is puzzled by what he has said and follows him. And despite the fact that she is often afraid of the brutal Sikes, she is in love with him.

It was nearly midnight when Fagin left Nancy, and he hurried home through the piercing cold night as quickly as he could. As he shivered, fumbling for his door key, he was startled by a man who inquired how his business of the night had gone. Inside in the darkness, Fagin fumbled down the dark kitchen staircase and returned with a candle and led the stranger upstairs. Once there, Fagin and the stranger, whom Fagin now called Monks, talked in whispers about Oliver and the robbery.

Monks, angry because Fagin had not kept Oliver and made him a pickpocket, was told by Fagin that the robbery was the only way Oliver could have been made one of the gang. Nervous and trembling, Monks proclaimed that what has happened to Oliver is in no way his fault because "I told you from the first, I won't shed blood." At this point, the two were startled by the shadow of a woman on the wall. Although they searched, they found nothing. Finally convinced by Fagin that it must have been his imagination, Monks left.

Comment

At this point, Monks, though important to the plot, remains a mystery. And so, by still another inventive device, Dickens holds the reader's attention.

CHAPTER TWENTY-SEVEN

Meanwhile back at the workhouse, Mr. Bumble waited patiently for Mrs. Corney to return. And as he waited, he again carefully surveyed all of Mrs. Corney's belongings. "He recounted the teaspoons, reweighed the sugar tongs," examined the condition of the furniture, and because he still did not hear Mrs. Corney returning, investigated the contents of her chest of drawers. In it he discovered a quantity of clothing of good quality and a small padlocked box which sounded as if it were filled with coins. A few moments later Mrs. Corney arrived, gasping for breath, and Mr. Bumble brought her a glass of peppermint and gin from a bottle he had found in the cupboard. Thus comforted, Mrs. Corney invited Mr. Bumble to drink with her, and the two sat close together discussing matters of mutual interest.

Nothing was said for a few moments when in response to Mrs. Corney's hint, Mr. Bumble suggested that they might marry since Mr. Slout, master of the workhouse, was dying, and that he, Mr. Bumble, hoped to succeed to that position. Mrs. Corney after two of three attempts to speak, finally accepted. Matters thus arranged, Mrs. Corney hinted that she had just learned something which she would reveal after they were married. And Mr. Bumble left for Mr. Sowerberry's to arrange for Old Sally's funeral.

A short while later at Mr. Sowerberry's, Mr. Bumble was surprised to find Noah Claypole lolling drunkenly at the kitchen table, and being fed oysters by Charlotte "which he condescended to swallow." Angrily Mr. Bumble ordered Noah to shut up the shop and to tell Mr. Sowerberry to send a coffin to the workhouse, and he banished Charlotte downstairs to the kitchen. These preparations made, Mr. Bumble set off for home.

Comment

The scene between Mr. Bumble and Mrs. Corney is meant to be contrasted with the scene between Charlotte and Noah. Although Mr. Bumble readily condemns holding hands and kissing, he does not include himself in that general condemnation. Nor does he bother to examine his own callous motivation for proposing to Mrs. Corney - a desire to add her material possessions to his own.

CHAPTER TWENTY-EIGHT

Carrying the wounded Oliver, Sikes fled his pursuers. Suddenly aware that they were gaining, he ordered Toby, who had managed to get some distance ahead, to help carry Oliver. And even though Toby was frightened of the pistol with which Sikes threatened him, he was more afraid of the pursuing mob, so he turned and ran off at full speed. Sikes, now alone, threw his cloak over Oliver and fled after Toby.

Comment

Chapter Twenty-eight returns to the action left incomplete in **Chapter Twenty-two**. And although other portions of the narrative have advanced beyond this point, Dickens is now ready to pursue the major thread of the plot again.

At almost the same moment that Sikes had left Oliver and fled, his pursuers, Giles and Brittles, the two servants who had raised the alarm, and a Tinker who had been sleeping in an outhouse, called back the Tinker's dogs and held a hurried conference. Each then revealed to the others his fear that they might actually catch up with the robbers. Each, with his admission revealed, sighed in relief, and they hurried home as quickly as they could. As a result, Oliver lay motionless and insensible throughout the cold and damp night where Sikes had left him.

At length, awakened by the rain and the pain in his left arm which was wrapped in a blood soaked shawl, Oliver raised himself painfully to a sitting position. Although he fell on his first attempt to stand, he struggled to his feet and stumbled off aimlessly into the darkness. Confused and helpless, he staggered along the road until he came to a house. But just as he was about to knock, he noted fearfully that it was the house they had attempted to rob. Although he was frightened and wanted to run, he staggered across the lawn, knocked faintly at the door and collapsed on the porch.

Inside, Giles and Brittles were recounting their brave adventures of the evening for the other servants in the kitchen. In the midst of their humorous and somewhat exaggerated tale, they were interrupted by the sound of a knock at the door.

Immediately an excited discussion followed over who should answer; it was finally decided that they would all open the door together. When the door was finally opened, the three beheld the unconscious Oliver, and carried him inside, and shouted wildly that they had caught one of the thieves. Upon hearing this, the young woman of the house, refusing to look at Oliver, ordered that he be put to bed and the doctor sent for.

| Comment |

As in Elizabethan tragedy, and in the melodramatic theater of Dickens' own day, tragic scenes were often relieved by comic scenes which followed. Undoubtedly, Dickens did not want the effect of his book to be totally oppressive. He wanted to keep his audience and he was able to do so with a comic with already proved successful in *Pickwick*.

A tinker was a traveling mender of kettles and pans.

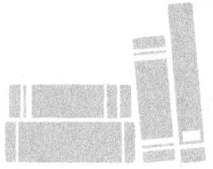

OLIVER TWIST

TEXTUAL ANALYSIS

CHAPTERS 29 - 38

CHAPTER TWENTY-NINE

Sometime later the two ladies of the house, the elderly Mrs. Maylie, and her lovely seventeen year old ward, Rose, waited in a handsome, well-furnished room for the arrival of the doctor, Mr. Losberne. Although Brittles had been sent over an hour before for the doctor, he still had not returned. Finally the doctor arrived. After paying his respects to the two ladies, and exchanging a few humorous pleasantries with Giles, he made his way up to the bedroom. The good doctor remained in the room much longer than either of the ladies had expected, and there was a good deal of activity as servants ran up and down the stairs carrying necessary items. At length the doctor came down, looking very mysterious. In response to a question about Oliver's condition, he asked if either of the ladies had seen the thief.

Informed by Mrs. Maylie that they had not, the doctor suggested that they go up to him. Accordingly, the doctor informed them that the patient was quiet and comfortable, and escorted them to the room where Oliver lay.

> Comment

Rose Maylie, like most of Dickens' heroines, is as pure and as innocent as any who have ever appeared in novels. In this case, however, Dickens was drawing a sentimental and idealized portrait of his sister-in-law, Mary Hogarth, who had recently died. Note the mysterious manner by which the doctor coaxes the ladies up to see Oliver, and Dickens, the reader, to the next chapter.

In this section of the story Oliver is once again extricated from Fagin's world. Both times when Oliver is transported into the good world there is an interval of unconsciousness between, followed by a period of serious illness. He awakes into a world where he can wander freely without danger; his dream becomes reality.

CHAPTER THIRTY

Assuring the ladies that they would be surprised, the doctor led the ladies, with much ceremony, upstairs. Looking first into the room to see if Oliver was in "visiting order," the doctor then mentioned for them to follow. Both of the ladies were surprised to behold the wounded Oliver, worn and exhausted, with his arm bound in a splint lying on the bed - not at all the "black-visaged ruffian they had expected." Rose, moved to tears by the sight, sat by the bedside and softly brushed Oliver's hair from his forehead as the kindly doctor and Mrs. Maylie watched. All found it difficult to believe that so fair and innocent a child could be a criminal, though the doctor feared it was possible.

Then leaving the room so that their conversation would not disturb the sleeping patient, the ladies pleaded with the doctor that some mercy be shown Oliver, to which plea the doctor replied that Oliver would be awake shortly and that he would question him to discover if he really was a "bad one." And more, the ladies agreed to accept as final whatever opinion the doctor offered as a result of that interview.

It was evening before Oliver was sufficiently recovered to undergo the interview, and the interview lasted longer than expected. Under the kindly doctor's questioning, Oliver, weak and in pain, feebly recounted the "evils and calamities" of his life. Until finally, the gentle doctor, his eyes filled with tears, watched as Oliver fell asleep again, and went downstairs to the kitchen. There Giles and Brittles were entertaining the women servants and the local constable, who had been called, with their adventures of the previous night. Here the doctor, refusing to drink, bullied Giles and Brittles into an admission that they could not truthfully testify that the wounded boy upstairs, and the robber they had shot at, were the same person. Then turning to the constable, the doctor pointed out carefully the consequences of that admission. At this moment, the confused scene was interrupted by Brittles' announcement that the Bow Street officers, who had been sent for late last night, had finally arrived.

Comment

In many respects this chapter introduces for discussion one of the critical questions raised by the novel. Although Oliver has never had any formal education, and although he has been exposed all his life to evil influences, he has somehow managed to remain totally innocent. In fact, even his speech is not like that of other boys whose experiences were similar. The laws of Victorian England were harsh. And if Oliver were not protected by the doctor, he would have been treated as if he were an adult criminal. In fact the punishment for robbery was death by hanging or by banishment to the British Empire's prison colony in Australia. (As in the case of Magwitch in *Great Expectations*.)

CHAPTER THIRTY-ONE

Brittles opened the door to admit the Bow Street officers and was confronted by a fat man in a heavy overcoat who ordered him to go outside and put away their gig (a light horse-drawn wagon) so that his partner might come in. This done, the two officers entered the parlor where they were greeted by Dr. Losberne. Here they announced themselves as Blathers, a stout man about fifty, and Duff, "a thin redheaded man with a sinister nose." They were greeted by the ladies, and listened as Dr. Losberne recounted the details of the robbery at great length. Having thus listened to the doctor's account, Blathers remarked that it was not the work of a "yokel," a term which Dr. Losberne translated for the ladies to mean a "country man."

But when the officers inquired about Oliver's connection with the attempted robbery, they were for a time put off by the doctor who explained that the servants' identification of Oliver was mistaken. Thus temporarily satisfied, the officers then set out to inspect the scene of the robbery, accompanied by the village constable. This done, they questioned Giles and Brittles, whose confused and contradictory accounts they heard six times over, during which time Dr. Losberne and the ladies determined to protect Oliver as best they could. And because Oliver's story might prove difficult, the doctor decided to tell the officers that he was too ill to be questioned. Thus, when the officers returned to question them, the ladies and the doctor supplied them with drinks and drew them into long and involved accounts of their many experiences as detectives. And while they talked the doctor slipped out of the room, returning shortly to inform them that Oliver could now be questioned.

In the bedroom Oliver stared seemingly without understanding at the officers while the doctor explained that Oliver had been wounded by some kind of a boy's spring gun. Again they questioned Giles who could not make a positive identification, nor could Brittles later in the next room. As a result, the officers, as suspicious of Giles' marksmanship as of his intelligence, inspected the other pistol which he had carried but had not fired. They discovered that although it was loaded and primed, it had no ball in it. This discovery, of course, impressed everyone except the doctor who had ten minutes before removed it.

The next morning the case was further complicated by the arrest of two men and a boy. But the only crime of which they could be proved guilty was sleeping in a haystack, a crime itself punishable by imprisonment. In any event, the case further confused, Mrs. Maylie and Dr. Losberne posted bail to insure that Oliver would appear if he were ever called. Blathers and Duff, richer by a couple of guineas, returned home, divided in opinion on the subject of crime. Meanwhile, Oliver grew better under the care of Mrs. Maylie, Rose and the doctor.

Comment

The officers, Blathers and Duff, are treated as humorously incompetent, as are the servants, Giles and Brittles. And so

Dickens satirizes not only the institution of Victorian law, but its representatives as well. The Bow Street officers were members of the Metropolitan, or London, police force who took charge of investigation beyond the capabilities of local constabulary, in London and its immediate suburbs.

CHAPTER THIRTY-TWO

In addition to his broken arm, Oliver had a fever, brought on by exposure to the wet and cold, which hung on for many weeks. But at length, he began to get better though much reduced by his illness. And finally, mostly recovered, he wished earnestly to in some way repay the kindness of Mrs. Maylie and Rose, who told him that they were going to take him on a trip to see Mr. Brownlow. Accordingly, a few days later, Oliver set out with Dr. Losberne in a small carriage. At Chertsey bridge Oliver noticed the deserted house to which Sikes had earlier brought him. At his cry, Dr. Losberne jumped from the carriage and ran to the front of the house and began to kick violently at the door. When it was suddenly opened by a small humpbacked man, the doctor grabbed him by the collar and held him fast. But the humpbacked man claimed angrily to have lived in the house for twenty-five years and protested that he had never heard of anyone named Sikes. Unable to secure any information, the doctor then gave the hunchback a coin to calm him and returned to the carriage, followed by the wild-eyed hunchback who glared fiercely into the carriage at Oliver.

Arriving finally in London, Oliver remembered the name of the street on which Mr. Brownlow had lived, and they drove straight there. But when they finally arrived at the house they found a "to let" sign in the window and the house empty.

Inquiring next door, they were told by a servant that "Mr. Brownlow had sold his goods and gone to the West Indies, six weeks before" with his housekeeper. Bitterly disappointed, they got back into the carriage and drove back to Chertsey.

A few weeks later spring finally came at last. Oliver, Mrs. Maylie and Rose left for a small cottage in the country. These were happy days for Oliver. For the first time, without care or fear, he spent happy hours learning to read from an old gentleman who lived nearby, sitting in the garden with the ladies talking, or listening to Rose play the piano and sing. And on Sundays, he went to church and read his Bible. Three pleasant months had smoothly passed by in this was and Oliver and the two ladies grew more and more attached to one another.

Comment

Fagin's gang has cleverly covered its tracks. The humpbacked man is, of course, another member of the gang. Note too that he is as ugly as his villainous associates.

CHAPTER THIRTY-THREE

As spring flew swiftly by, and summer came, Oliver grew strong and healthy. However, one evening after returning from a walk, Rose announced to Oliver and Mrs. Maylie that she was ill. She, like Oliver earlier, had contracted a very dangerous fever. Although grief stricken and worried, Mrs. Maylie bore this new misfortune firm in the belief that "Heaven is just," and sent Oliver to town (some four miles distant) with a letter to Dr. Losberne at Chertsey. With it Oliver ran across the fields as fast as he could until he arrived out of breath at the marketplace of the market-town. Here after many inquiries, he found the local inn and arranged with the landlord to have the letter sent by the first stage. But as Oliver turned to leave the inn he accidentally bumped into a tall man wrapped in a cloak who cursed at him strangely, and then fell in a fit upon the ground. Supposing him to be a madman, Oliver secured help for him in the inn and hurried back to Rose and Mrs. Maylie.

Rose had rapidly grown worse and by midnight a local doctor announced that it would be "a miracle, if she recovered." And thus, for many days Rose lay near death. Into the quiet cottage visitors came and left, and Dr. Losberne finally arrived to confirm the opinion of the local doctor. As the fear and suspense mounted, Oliver one morning prayed in the peaceful pleasant surroundings of the local churchyard. Here interrupted by the tolling of the churchbell summoning yet another person to heaven, Oliver turned homeward where he was surprised to find Mrs. Maylie alone in the parlor. Fearing that Rose had died, he learned instead that Rose had fallen into a deep coma from which she would either recover or die. They sat there quietly for hours, until their vigil was interrupted by Dr. Losberne who told them the good news that Rose would live "for years to come."

Comment

Among Dickens' best writing were his famous deathbed scenes (Paul Dombey in *Dombey and Son*, Little Nell in *The Old Curiosity Shop* are good examples), but on this occasion his allowing Rose to live reflects perhaps his deepest felt wish that his own young sister-in-law, Mary Hogarth, might have lived.

Again the plot is advanced by the device of coincidence. For Oliver's accidental meeting with the cloaked man (Monks) is a **foreshadowing** of events to come.

CHAPTER THIRTY-FOUR

Stunned by the unexpected news, Oliver was unable to speak or even weep until he had walked for more than an hour in the quiet evening. Then he burst into tears and turned homeward. As he walked he was interrupted by the sound of a familiar voice asking for news of Rose. It was Giles, driving the chaise dressed in his nightgown and bringing Harry Maylie, Mrs. Maylie's son. Upon receipt of the news that Rose was better, Harry got out of the carriage and walked with Oliver to the cottage while Giles rode ahead.

Upset because Mrs. Maylie had not written sooner, Harry then told his mother of his determination to marry Rose, and Mrs. Maylie warned the love-smitten Harry that the "stain" of Rose's birth would be likely to cause Rose to refuse. She did, however, agree that Rose deserved "the best and purest love the heart of man can offer." In any case, under the cheerful influence of Harry and the doctor, Rose began to improve. Oliver, feeling better, went about his usual occupations, joined now by Harry, with renewed hope and pleasure. However, one evening he was disturbed in his dream by visions of Fagin calling to him. And awakening with a start, he saw at the window before him, the faces of the angry Fagin and the man who had accosted him at the inn staring in at him. In an instant they were gone and Oliver called loudly for help.

Comment

Moral standards in the Victorian period were, of course, much stricter than our own. Although Rose was innocent of any wrong doing, the illegitimacy of her birth was considered a "stain" which no marriage or association could wash away. Thus Mrs. Maylie was not being unkind, but merely reminding Harry of the burden he would be under if he married Rose.

Note the high point of suspense which the author reaches at the conclusion of this (the fifteenth) installment of the book. Dickens had no mercy for the nerves of his readers!

CHAPTER THIRTY-FIVE

Although the inmates of the house hurried to Oliver's side and pursued the fleeing criminals, they were unable to catch them. Giles, who had been sent to the village to inquire if any strangers had been seen, was also unable to secure any further information. Not only had the two men vanished, but they had vanished without having left so much as a footprint, and after a few days, the affair was forgotten.

Meanwhile Rose recovered rapidly, and was able to again join the family. However, in spite of the happiness caused by her appearance, there was a strange restraint also, and more than once Rose appear d with "tears on her face." Finally one morning Harry visited Rose, alone at breakfast, told her how much he loved her, and urged her to marry him. Although Rose admitted that she loved him, her eyes filled with tears. She refused because she was a "portionless girl, with a blight on my name." Had Harry been poor and penniless, she admitted, she might have married him, but as things were now she could not. Harry, promising to lay all at her feet, vowed to ask again in a year, and left the room.

Comment

The scene between Rose and Harry reveals well the difference between tragedy and melodrama. In tragedy the obstacles which separate lovers cannot be overcome, in melodrama they only seem impossible to overcome. Thus although the scene appears old-fashioned to the modern reader, the Victorian reader not only expected it but wept over it. To the modern reader the conflict has a soap-opera quality, with the implicit question, "Will love conquer all?"

CHAPTER THIRTY-SIX

The next morning before the ladies were up, Harry had breakfast with Oliver and Dr. Losberne. Informing the doctor of his intention to return to Chertsey with him, Harry then revealed that he planned to see a rich and powerful uncle who wanted to get him into Parliament. At that moment Giles arrived with the chaise, and began to load the luggage. Harry took Oliver aside and asked him to write and keep him informed about Rose. Honored, Oliver promised to do so and Harry mounted the chaise with the doctor and rode off. Through a latticed window, Harry caught a glimpse of the tearful Rose, and he commanded Giles to drive "hard, fast, full gallop."

Comment

Money and position were more important in certain segments of Victorian society than they are in our own. It was quite likely that Harry's uncle would seek a parliamentary appointment for him, for next to one's own honor, a Victorian gentleman considered his family's.

CHAPTER THIRTY-SEVEN

Meanwhile back at the workhouse, Mr. Bumble, by now married for two months to Mrs. Corney, sat gloomily meditating upon the mistake he had made in giving up his position as beadle to marry Mrs. Corney and become master of the workhouse. Undermined by his wife and ruled by the new beadle and his assistant, Mr. Bumble grumbled loudly about having sold himself "cheap." He was unfortunately overheard by Mrs. Bumble, who resorted to tears. But when these failed to produce the desired effect in the brutish Bumble, she angrily scratched his face, pushed him over a chair, and chased him, surprised and beaten, from the house. Later wandering about the workhouse and the yard, Mr. Bumble reflected for the first time upon injustice. He was again rebuffed by Mrs. Bumble, and he left angrily for town.

In town he entered a nearly deserted public house and sat near a tall, dark, cloaked stranger who nodded and the two drank for some time in silence. Finally the stranger inquired if Mr. Bumble had once been the beadle. To which Mr. Bumble assented and said he was now master of the workhouse. The stranger then informed Mr. Bumble that he had come to see him because he wanted some information. He bought Mr. Bumble a drink. Admitting he was interested in money, Mr. Bumble pocketed the coins which the dark man offered and listened as the man asked him to remember back "twelve years last winter." The man inquired then about the circumstances of Oliver's birth and of the whereabouts of Old Sally who had attended that birth.

Alarmed by Mr. Bumble's answers the stranger prepared to depart, but was detained by Mr. Bumble, who sensing profit, informed the stranger that his wife had some further information. It was then arranged that Mrs. Bumble and the stranger, who said his name was Monks, should meet the next day.

BRIGHT NOTES STUDY GUIDE

Comment

For the full effect of Dickens' ironic **satire**, this chapter should be compared with the previous one. Compare the ideal and innocent love of Harry and Rose with the greedy and grasping arrangement between Mr. Bumble and Mrs. Corney.

Bumble gets his final comeuppance in this chapter. He is finally shorn of his authority, his cocked hat (the symbol of the beadle's position), and his masculine supremacy in his own home. Vanity has been replaced by a grudging resignation to his hen-pecking wife. Later, in **Chapter Fifty-one** when Mr. Brownlow tells Bumble that the law supposes that his wife acts under his direction, Bumble replies: "If that's the eye of the law, the law is a bachelor."

CHAPTER THIRTY-EIGHT

The next evening Mr. and Mrs. Bumble, dressed in shabby clothes, set out for their meeting with Monks. Later in a shabby district near the river, after consulting an address on a piece of paper, they entered a ruined building and were greeted by Monks. As they prepared to ascend to the second floor, loud claps of nearby thunder caused Monks to shrink back and cover his face with his hands. When he uncovered his face the Bumbles were frightened to see it distorted and discolored, but were reassured by Monks, who explained that he was subject to fits brought on my thunder.

Monks recovered and the three proceeded to an attic room where they bargained for Mrs. Bumble's information. Finally in spite of Monk's protest, they agreed on twenty-five pounds, but Mrs. Bumble would not reveal what Old Sally had told her until the money was paid. Monks reluctantly handed over the money. Mrs. Bumble then revealed that Old Sally had kept something which Oliver's mother had asked her to keep for her child just before she died. And Mrs. Bumble had found a pawn ticket in Old Sally's hand which she had redeemed for a gold locket, containing two locks of hair, and a gold wedding ring engraved with the name "Agnes" and a date a year earlier than Oliver's birth. She then gave Monks a small kid bag containing these articles. Monks, apparently satisfied because he made no attempt to take back his twenty-five pounds, refused to answer Mrs. Bumble's questions concerning his interest in these matters, and revealed that the Bumbles had been seated over a trapdoor during the interview. Through the trapdoor he then dropped Mrs. Bumble's packet which landed with a splash in the river below and was gone. Frightened and intimidated by Monks' strange manner, the Bumbles agreed to keep silent, and went home. After they had left, Monks called to a boy who had been hidden below and the two returned to the room where Monks had questioned Mrs. Bumble.

Comment

Again Dickens employs the trappings of melodrama. The old house, the storm, the violently distorted and discolored face of Monks, and the trapdoor are melodramatic devices borrowed partly from the gothic novel and partly from the stage. Note too Dickens' characteristic habit of making his criminals totally unattractive.

The ring and the locket are, of course, articles by which Oliver's past might be traced. Although they have been disposed of, knowledge of their existence has not. In addition to Monks and the Bumbles, remember the two old crones who were listening at the door in **Chapter Twenty-four.**

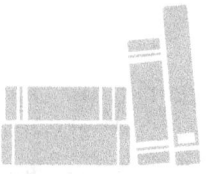

OLIVER TWIST

TEXTUAL ANALYSIS

CHAPTERS 39 - 53

CHAPTER THIRTY-NINE

Since his escape at Chertsey, Bill Sikes had lain ill in his room, tended by Nancy who had by now pawned everything of value to keep him alive. The two, much altered by their ordeal, were finally visited by Fagin, the Artful Dodger, and Charley Bates on the night after Monks' encounter with the Bumbles. Bringing wine and food, they were surprised to find Nancy and Sikes in such desperate circumstances, but the wine and the food soon produced an improvement in the pair's physical well-being, if not in Sikes' temper. Sikes, angry because he had been so long ignored, demanded money from Fagin and dispatched Nancy with him to bring it.

At Fagin's den they found Toby Crackit and Tom Chitling gambling at cards. Toby, since he had won all the money Tom had, prepared then to leave, followed shortly by Tom, the Dodger and Charley Bates, whom Fagin sent out. As soon as they left, Fagin produced a key and was about to get some money when they were interrupted by a man's voice on the staircase. And after Nancy had hidden her bonnet and shawl beneath the table, the man (who proved to be Monks) was admitted by Fagin. Pretending not to listen, Nancy watched the two men carefully; when they went upstairs, she followed quietly to listen.

Later when Fagin came down he noted how pale Nancy was, but she retorted that there was nothing wrong, took the money which Fagin reluctantly offered and left. Outside she sat down bewildered for a time on the doorstep, and suddenly arose and ran off in the direction opposite that of Sikes' place. However, soon out of breath, she stopped, burst into tears and hurried back toward Sikes. Although Sikes growled his satisfaction because she had brought money, he took no notice of her agitation. But later that evening, Sikes, as he demanded his fourth glass of hot water and gin, noticed Nancy's paleness and demanded to know "what's the matter." Then satisfied that she was only ill with fever, he drank his gin - into which Nancy had secretly slipped laudanum - and soon fell asleep. At this, Nancy, "like one who is on the eve of some bold and hazardous step," dressed nervously and left.

Outside she walked swiftly towards the West-End of London. Here she entered a quiet family hotel near Hyde Park, and asked uncertainly to see Rose Maylie. And after some difficulty with the night clerk and some servants who were disturbed by her shabby appearance, a message was sent up and Nancy was taken upstairs to a small antechamber.

Comment

Although Nancy loves Sikes and is afraid of the gang, she has now determined to help Oliver. Laudanum was an opium mixture commonly used as a pain killer in the nineteenth century.

CHAPTER FORTY

Inside, Nancy, her feelings still struggling with her pride, was interrupted by Rose who asked what she wanted. Then Nancy, in tears because of Rose's kindness, related the story of her life of vice including her kidnapping of Oliver. Rose listened impatiently as Nancy told of Monks' bargain with Fagin and of their conversation in which Nancy had heard of her. Puzzled because she knew no person named Monks, Rose listened in astonishment as Nancy revealed that Monks had paid Fagin to make Oliver a thief, and that Monks had disposed of the ring and the locket, which were the only proof of Oliver's real identity, because Oliver was his brother. Nancy further related Monks' hatred of Rose and Mrs. Maylie and of Monks' dark hint of having the "young devil's money safely now," for it would be worth "thousands and hundreds of pounds" if Rose and Mrs. Maylie knew who Oliver really was.

Frightened because she had been gone so long Nancy prepared to leave, but was restrained by Rose who, fearful for Nancy's safety, arranged for Nancy to meet with her and a kind gentleman friend on Sunday between eleven and twelve on London Bridge. Although Nancy refused Rose's kind offer of shelter because she could not desert Bill, she agreed to meet them on the bridge "if I am alive."

Comment

This chapter, crucial to the main plot of the novel, reveals one of the great flaws of the plot. For although Nancy reveals that Monks had first seen Oliver in **Chapters Ten** and **Eleven**, there is no mention of him on those occasions. Thus, because of the difficulties of serial publication and the deliberate withholding of information from the reader, *Oliver Twist* has, like many of Dickens' serial publications, serious flaws in its plot.

CHAPTER FORTY-ONE

Though touched by Nancy's concern for Oliver, and eager to know the mystery of Oliver's birth, Rose, not wanting to betray Nancy's confidence, wondered what she should do during her three remaining days in London. Afraid that Dr. Losberne might be impetuous, and reluctant to call Harry, she spent a sleepless night. However, the next morning she was interrupted by Oliver, who brought the news that Mr. Brownlow had returned. Realizing that Mr. Brownlow might be the answer to her problem, Rose quickly called a coach and went to see him. Arriving there she was conducted upstairs to Mr. Brownlow and Mr. Grimwig.

Rose then told the surprised and agitated gentlemen that she brought news of Oliver Twist, and told them what she could of Oliver's kidnapping, omitting Nancy's part in it. Mr. Brownlow, in spite of Mr. Grimwig's dark warnings, was overjoyed, even more so when he discovered that Oliver was in the carriage below. In a few moments, Mr. Brownlow, joined by Mrs. Bedwin, was joyfully reunited with Oliver. And a short while later Mr. Brownlow left Oliver with Mrs. Bedwin, listened to Rose's narrative of her interview with Nancy, and arranged to meet with her at eight o'clock that evening.

At Rose's hotel later that evening, Mr. Brownlow, after persuading Dr. Losberne to restrain himself, advised that they should proceed with caution. He suggested further that Monks could only be defeated by carefully planned strategy, if the mystery of Oliver's birth was to be solved. With Mrs. Maylie's and Rose's approval, Dr. Losberne was forced to accept Mr.

Brownlow's proposition, and agree that Mr. Grimwig and Harry Maylie be added to their group. It was further agreed that Rose remain in London as long as necessary. Accordingly, preparations were made by them to meet Nancy.

Comment

Note how several plot strands are brought together by the device of coincidence in this chapter. Not only does Oliver accidentally meet Mr. Brownlow, who has fortunately returned from the West Indies, but coincidentally Rose, Mrs. Maylie, and Oliver just happened to be in London.

The eighteenth installment of the novel concludes here. Once again there is a **climax** of suspense to be left hanging, while Dickens abruptly shifts the scene to some old acquaintances, Noah and Charlotte.

CHAPTER FORTY-TWO

On the same evening as Rose's meeting with Nancy, two people advanced toward London on the Great North Road. The knock-kneed and boney man proved to be Noah Claypole, and his robust companion who was carrying the bulk of their luggage, Charlotte. Having stolen money from Mr. Sowerberry's till, they fled toward the safety of London. Cross and tired, they finally stopped at a small, dirty, public house, the Three Cripples, to spend the night. Here they were ushered into a small back room by Barney, who informed them that lodgings were available and brought them food. As they ate, they were watched through a small window by the landlord of the tavern. A few minutes later Fagin entered the tavern on his usual evening rounds and was informed by Barney that Noah appeared to be a suitable pupil for Fagin's business. Accordingly, Fagin stationed himself at the window and listened to Charlotte and Noah intently. Overhearing Noah's boast about being a great thief, Fagin interrupted, admitted that he had overheard Noah and offered to help them advance in the "business." Though somewhat surprised, Noah sent Charlotte upstairs and accepted Fagin's offer, and paid twenty pounds of the money he had stolen for Fagin's help. Noah thought, however, that he should be trained for such light work as spying, or stealing from small children (as Fagin had jestingly suggested), since Charlotte would "be able to do a good deal." Then introducing himself and Charlotte, who had returned, as Mr. and Mrs. Bolter, Noah agreed to meet Fagin at ten the next morning at Fagin's den.

Comment

Although the sudden coincidental introduction of Charlotte and Noah does little to advance the plot, it serves to provide some relief for the tragic scenes to come. Note too that the name Bolter aptly describes Charlotte and Noah at this stage.

CHAPTER FORTY-THREE

The next morning at Fagin's den, Fagin informed Noah that a criminal must take care of "Number One," which in the gang meant all of them, because if one were caught, they might all hang. He then gave Noah a detailed description of the gang's operations, adding, to further impress Noah with the proper respect and fear, that he had lost his "best hand … yesterday morning." For not only had the Artful Dodger been arrested as a pickpocket, but a silver snuff box had been found in his pocket. Although he reflected that the Dodger might be imprisoned for only a few weeks if the prosecutor were careless, Fagin believed that the Dodger would be transported for life. Interrupted by Charley Bates, who informed him that witnesses would be forthcoming to identify the Dodger in court, Fagin humored Charley with a description of how the Dodger would humorously defend himself in the courtroom. And Charley, caught up in Fagin's imaginative portrait, forgot for the moment the seriousness of the Dodger's situation.

With some difficulty Fagin then persuaded Charley not to go to the Dodger's trial himself and suggested that Noah, who was not known to the London police, be sent instead, dressed as a waggoner. Although Noah protested, arrangements were quickly made and Noah soon found himself in the crowded dirty Bow Street court. Here Noah watched the quick disposition of the previous case; then the Dodger was brought in. And the Dodger, still in character, despite his predicament, demanded to know why he was being placed in a "disgraceful sitivation" since he was an Englishman who demanded his "privileges." Throughout the proceedings which followed, the Dodger made a complete shambles of the judicial proceedings with his defense, closing before his sentence with a threat to take his case before the House of Commons. Finally, however, the Dodger was "fully committed," and led off to jail. Noah then hurried back to Fagin with the news that the Dodger had done "full justice to his upbringing."

Comment

Compare this courtroom scene with the one in **Chapter Eleven**. Again Dickens, who had been a court reporter, directs his **satire** at the legal system which denies its victims due process of law. Dickens lets the Dodger command the scene, who, in his own crude manner, makes some acute comments about the legal system.

CHAPTER FORTY-FOUR

Nancy, struggling desperately with the conflict raised by her pledge to Rose, and her loyalty to Sikes, grew pale, thin, and distraught. Finally on the appointed Sunday evening she sat, listening distractedly to Sikes and Fagin when the clock struck eleven. She then prepared to leave, but she was interrupted by Sikes, who demanded to know where she was going. And Sikes, not satisfied by her explanations, forced her to stay and locked the door. Hysterically she struggled and protested, and then left the room for a time while Sikes and Fagin discussed her strange behavior.

Later as Fagin left, and Nancy lighted his way downstairs with a candle, he attempted to find out what was bothering her, but she gave no information. And as Fagin walked home alone, he wondered if Nancy had found another lover who might be valuable to him in getting rid of Sikes who knew too much. Thus speculating and suspicious, he decided to have Nancy watched as a means of increasing his influence over her.

Comment

Fagin's suspicious and devious nature will cause Nancy's downfall.

CHAPTER FORTY-FIVE

The next morning at breakfast Fagin completed his arrangements for having Nancy watched. Artfully flattering the foolish Noah, Fagin promised him a pound to shadow Nancy, and he agreed. For six weary nights Noah waited in his waggoner's disguise for

Fagin's word to go, and finally on the seventh, Sunday again, he was given instructions to go. Noah then followed Fagin to the Three Cripples where Nancy was pointed out to him, and he followed her at a cautious distance when she left.

Comment

Noah is, of course, ideal for this task since he is the only member of the gang not known to Nancy. Fagin's decision to have Nancy followed is typical of his method of survival. He always commits evil by proxy. He never partakes in crime or death, but leads others to destruction. They form a wall between him and society, a wall that Nancy, one of his victims, eventually causes to crumble.

CHAPTER FORTY-SIX

As the church clock chimed a quarter to twelve, Nancy, still followed by Noah, crossed London Bridge anxiously peering at passersby. Apparently disappointed, she suddenly turned back across the bridge and nearly caught Noah. Shortly after midnight, as Nancy walked to and fro, a hackney-carriage stopped nearby and a young lady and a gray-haired gentleman dismounted and walked towards Nancy. Afraid to speak there, Nancy led them down some nearby steps on the Surrey bank. Noah, who had hastened ahead of them, concealed himself below. From his vantage point Noah listened as Nancy related her fears and explained that she did not come last Sunday because she had been "kept by force." Finally she told them that she had drugged "him" (Sikes), and listened as Mr. Brownlow asked her help to extort Monks' secret from him. She refused to deliver up Fagin for fear it might involve Sikes, but she did agree to put Monks into Mr. Brownlow's hands if Fagin were not brought to justice without her consent.

Willing to take Mr. Brownlow's word, Nancy described the Three Cripples which Monks often frequented and described him, adding finally, that he had a mark upon his throat. At this Mr. Brownlow cried "a broad red mark, like a burn or a scald?" Although it was apparent that Mr. Brownlow had recognized Monks as someone he knew from Nancy's description, he would say no more. Mr. Brownlow then offered Nancy "a quiet asylum" away from her associates wherever she wished, but Nancy refused. For though she hated and loathed her life, it was now too late to change, even though she knew that sooner or later she would be likely to end her life in the dark river. Then refusing any payment for her help, Nancy asked them to leave and watched until they were out of sight. Crying bitterly, she left herself. When she had gone the astonished Noah ran toward Fagin's place as fast as he could.

Comment

This chapter adds greatly to the melodramatic quality of the novel. For not only are characters from practically every stage of Oliver's life present, but the plot is advanced by a theatrical device as old as the theater, the eavesdropper. Note too, Dickens' effective use of description to evoke mood. The bridge, the dark river, and the gloomy night are all suitable as a backdrop for the drama enacted on the bridge.

CHAPTER FORTY-SEVEN

Just before dawn, Fagin sat crouched over the cold hearth at his den brooding hideously over Nancy's deception. Noah slept on the floor before him. At last Fagin was interrupted by the arrival of Sikes who was amazed by Fagin's violently distraught appearance. Hesitant and agitated, Fagin then asked Sikes what he would do if any of the gang were to inform on them. When Sikes responded violently, Fagin awoke Noah and drew from him the story of Nancy's betrayal. Sikes sprang violently to the door, ignoring Fagin's attempts to calm him, and dashed out into the street. Headlong he plunged toward his own place and there quietly opened the door and approached the bed.

He awakened the half-dressed Nancy and dragged her, frightened and surprised, to the middle of the room, his hands on her head and throat. Telling her she had been watched, he ignored her pleas to spare her life because she had not betrayed him. Nor would he listen to her pleas for him to join her in the refuge Mr. Brownlow had promised. Instead, maddened beyond reason, Sikes grasped his pistol (though at the last moment did not fire for fear of the noise it would make), and beat with all his force on her upturned face. And as Nancy, dazed and blinded with blood, held a handkerchief to her face and gasped out a prayer, he seized a heavy club and struck her down.

Comment

This chapter, containing the death of Nancy, is one of the most famous Dickens ever wrote, and was often included as a part of his public readings many years later.

When Dickens wrote these last few chapters, he was still passionately influenced by the death of Mary Hogarth a few months before. In fact, he told his wife Kate that "after she died, I dreamed of her every night for months."

This scene is a startlingly dramatic presentation of Sikes' brutality. Fagin, the deceptive betrayer, would never have been capable of either this blind fury or such a brutal murder. Nancy's death flows with inexorable logic from her choice to defend such a brute. Our sympathy with her dreadful plight makes Sikes' villainy even more hateful.

CHAPTER FORTY-EIGHT

The next morning Sikes, terrified by what he had done, sat staring at Nancy's bloody body. Finally he rose, burned the club and attempted to clean the blood from the room and from his clothes. At length, dragging his dog with him, unable to take his eyes off Nancy, he backed out of the room, locked the door and left the house. Not sure where to go, Sikes fled swiftly out of London, but soon turned back again by another road, and wandered about for many hours. Finally by nine in the evening, he stopped at a small tavern at Hatfield where he sat down in the furthest corner to eat and drink. He had almost fallen asleep when a peddler who sold stain removers, entered noisily and seized Sikes' hat to demonstrate its efficacy in removing all kinds of stain, including "bloodstains." Angrily Sikes grabbed his hat, overturned the table and fled.

Outside he saw the London coach waiting, and he walked over to it to see what news the passengers might have. And hearing news of murder of Spitalfields, he rushed out of town, believing he could see Nancy's ghost following wherever he went. Desperately he fled, attempting to lose the ghostly figure, but everywhere it followed. Finally he lay shivering in a dark shed, Nancy's eyes staring at him in the dark, when he heard the cry of "fire." Rushing out he discovered a barn on fire and he remained to help fight the fire. The excitement of the fire over, Sikes' fear returned when he heard the firemen discussing the murder; he called his dog and fled.

Aware now that the police were searching for him, and afraid of being alone, he impulsively turned toward London. Then suddenly aware that his dog might give him away, he decided to drown him, but the animal, instinctively recognizing his danger, ran away. Although Sikes waited, the dog did not return and at length he resumed the journey.

Comment

Although Sikes has not yet been caught, his punishment has already begun. Note too, that although Sikes had heretofore been a totally unredeemed villain, he now assumes a more human quality.

CHAPTER FORTY-NINE

Early that same evening Mr. Brownlow had Monks brought to his house where he was offered two choices. He could either tell Mr. Brownlow what he wanted to know, or be arrested for fraud and robbery. And although Monks protested violently, Mr. Brownlow reminded Monks that he had no alternative, for the only thing which restrained Mr. Brownlow from calling the police was his old friendship for Monks' father. At this, Monks, really Edward Leeford, related the story of his father's forced marriage to an older woman. After Monks' birth his father and mother soon separated, and he and his mother had gone abroad to live. Afterward Monks' father had met and fallen in love with the beautiful young daughter of a retired naval officer. Although she and Monks' father were engaged, Monks' father found it necessary to go to Rome to handle the estate of a wealthy relative who had died there. In Rome, Mr. Brownlow revealed, Monks' father had himself died, leaving no will so that Monks and his mother had inherited his money. Then Mr. Brownlow informed the surprised Monks that Monks' father had visited him before his trip to Rome and had left behind a portrait of the girl he loved, and confided his intention to convert his property into cash and fly the country with her. Although Mr. Brownlow had sought the girl after his friend's death, he was unable to find her because the family had moved.

Years later after his rescue of Oliver, Mr. Brownlow related, he had noted the resemblance between Oliver and the portrait, but before he could learn more, Oliver had been kidnapped. Even then suspecting Monks, Mr. Brownlow had sought him without success in the West Indies where he had last been heard of. But recently, Mr. Brownlow now informed the surprised Monks, he had learned Oliver's whole story and Monks' part in it. Now Monks, thoroughly frightened, admitted everything and promised to repeat his story before witnesses, and to restore the portion of Oliver's fortune which he still held.

As Monks paced up and down seeking some avenue of escape, Dr. Losberne arrived with news that Sikes' dog had been seen and that he would soon be captured. Mr. Brownlow then offered a reward of fifty pounds to the man who captured Sikes, made arrangements for Monks to be brought to the Maylies' and left to join the search.

Comment

The loose ends of the plot are now gathered. For the first time the reader knows Monks' real identity, and the way is prepared for the story's climax.

CHAPTER FIFTY

In a ruinous house, located in the dilapidated and crumbling warehouse district called Jacobs Island, near the Thames, Toby Crackit, Tom Chitling and a recently returned convict named Kags hid from the police who were now looking for Fagin's friends. Fagin and Noah had already been caught; and Bet, who had discovered Nancy's body, had been taken in a straight jacket to the hospital. Now most of the old hideouts were searched and the gang scattered. As the three sat in silence, they were interrupted by the arrival of Sikes' dog, and were afraid Sikes might follow. Their fears were realized when Sikes knocked, and demanded admittance. Uneasily they answered Sikes' questions, until they were again interrupted by the arrival of Charley Bates, who screamed "murderer" at the sight of Sikes. Charley was soon silenced by the more powerful man. However, Charley, released at the sound of an approaching crowd, screamed again for help. But Sikes again grasped him, leaned out and shouted defiantly at the crowd.

Sikes then called for a rope, intending to escape out a rear window into a tidal ditch. Clutching the rope, he climbed out on to the roof. Here he saw that the ditch was empty because the tide was out. But responding to the angry cries of the crowd who now surrounded the warehouse, and had already broken in, Sikes fastened his rope around a chimney and prepared to lower himself into the muddy ditch, hoping to get away by swift action. But as he began to lower himself, the rope looped around his waist, he looked back toward the roof, threw his hands over his head and uttered a yell of terror, "the eyes again." As he tumbled off the parapet, the noose tightened about his neck and he fell about thirty-five feet, stopping with a sudden jerk. As Sikes hung there lifeless, Charley called for the crowd to take him out and Sikes' dog howled dismally on the parapet. Then attempting to jump to the dead man's shoulder, the dog missed and fell to his death in the ditch.

> Comment

Appropriately, and grotesquely Sikes has paid for his own grotesque crime. Note too the death of Sikes' dog, an event generally regarded by critics as a bit too melodramatic even for this melodramatic novel.

CHAPTER FIFTY-ONE

Two days later Oliver, accompanied by Mrs. Maylie, Rose, Dr. Losberne and Mrs. Bedwin, and followed by Mr. Brownlow and Monks, traveled toward his native town. As they rode, he pointed out the landmarks of his childhood, and thought again of his promise to Little Dick. Finally they stopped at the chief hotel where they were greeted by Mr. Grimwig, and there had dinner. After dinner Monks was brought in and forced to tell the story of his deception and to admit that Oliver was the illegitimate son of his father Edwin Leeford and of Agnes Fleming. Monks also revealed that he and his mother had found among his father's effects a letter to Agnes, confessing that he could not marry her because he had a wife, and a will leaving the bulk of his fortune to Agnes and her child. If the child should be a girl, she would inherit unconditionally, if a boy, only if he had not committed a wrong act before he became a man. If he had, the will provided in such case that the money would revert to Monks. Monks then admitted that his mother had burned the will and had kept the letter in case the girl's family should ever return. She then told the story to Agnes' father who died shortly after, believing Agnes had killed herself. Later when she was dying, Monks' mother had told him her secret and made him swear that if the girl still lived and a child had been born he would "hunt it down, and never let it rest."

The rest of Monks' story of the locket and the ring was confirmed by the arrival of Mr. and Mrs. Bumble, who denied any implication. They were quickly refuted by the two old crones, produced by Mr. Brownlow, who testified that they had watched Mrs. Bumble take the pawn ticket from Old Sally. The Bumbles, defiantly admitting their part in Monks' efforts, were ushered out as Mr. Brownlow promised that never again would they "be employed in a situation of trust."

These matters completed, Mr. Brownlow asked Monks if he knew Rose, to which Monks responded "yes," and then he forced Monks to tell what had happened to Agnes' father's younger daughter. Monks then related how the child was taken by some poor cottagers after her father's death to be reared. But Monks' mother had found the child and told the family that she was illegitimate, but the child was taken from them by a local widow who took pity on her. Of course, Mrs. Maylie was that widow and Rose was now revealed as Oliver's aunt. At this point Harry Maylie arrived and reminded Rose of her promise to consider his proposal of marriage. Determined now to become a clergyman, Harry swept aside her objection, and she accepted him. However, despite the happy situation Oliver faced one great disappointment - "poor Dick was dead."

Comment

Oliver's story is now complete and the complex plot virtually played out. Though in spite of its often sharply satiric social criticism, the novel more resembles a fairy tale than a novel. Not only is Oliver rescued, but he is rich. It remains for a later, greater Dickens novel for a complete statement of his belief concerning the acquisition of wealth, and the making of a gentleman. That novel is, of course, *Great Expectations*.

CHAPTER FIFTY-TWO

The courtroom was crowded at Fagin's trial, and Fagin sat attentive but mute as the judge charged the jury. As he waited for the verdict, he thought of the horrors of the gallows and the scaffold, and later, gazed sightless and haggard as the judge pronounced the sentence of death by hanging. Alone in his cell he thought through the dark night about the men he had watched die on the scaffold, until maddened with fear, he beat upon the bars and screamed despairingly. On the day of his execution as the time grew near, he cowered, bloodless, near his bed, and burning with fever he counted the moments. Visited by Oliver and Mr. Brownlow, Fagin at first did not know them, but finally recognized them and begged forgiveness and asked Oliver to pray for him. Oliver prayed that "God forgive this wretched man" as the prison attendants dragged him from Fagin's grasp and left the prison weeping, accompanied by Mr. Brownlow past the assembled crowd near the already erected scaffold.

Comment

Dickens' early interest in crime and criminals was to last all his life. Perhaps no other Victorian novelist had so great an understanding or sympathy for those condemned to die. Fagin, like Sikes, becomes at the hour of death not an object of scorn, but of pity. Dickens shrewdly makes Fagin's suffering more mental than physical. He was a man of wit and imagination; therefore he has to spend his last hours imagining his death.

CHAPTER FIFTY-THREE

Three months later Rose and Harry were married and Mrs. Maylie went to live with them. Mr. Brownlow adopted Oliver and took a cottage nearby, where they were often visited by Mr. Grimwig and Dr. Losberne. The doctor had returned to his practice in Chertsey, but soon left his practice and also took a cottage nearby. Monks, generously given half of Oliver's fortune, left for the new world where he squandered it and spent his remaining years in prison.

Noah Claypole, pardoned because he had testified against Fagin, and Charlotte turned informers and made their livelihood tricking tavernkeepers into giving them liquor after hours and then pocketing the reward for informing on them. And Mr. and Mrs. Bumble, now paupers and shorn of all authority, became inmates of the same workhouse they had once ruled. Charley Bates gave up crime and was now a farmer's shepherd. All the characters accounted for, the novel closes with the notation that a marble tablet bearing the name "Agnes" now stands in the village churchyard, though she is not buried there.

Comment

In Victorian novels it was customary to include a chapter which detailed what happened later to most of the characters. Such a chapter is, of course, highly artificial, and almost never included in modern novels.

OLIVER TWIST

CHARACTER ANALYSES

Like most of Dickens' novels *Oliver Twist* is filled with numerous memorable characters. The following is an analysis of the major characters followed by an alphabetical listing of others with an analysis of their relative importance to the story.

OLIVER TWIST

The novel's youthful hero. Although he has been reared in a workhouse, and apprenticed to thieves, he remains unchanged by his experiences. Forced to participate in a burglary, he is wounded, but recovers under the care of the Maylies. And through the intervention of Nancy, the plot against him is fully revealed, and he is restored to his rightful place in society.

Oliver's characterization is flat and two-dimensional. He is a symbolic figure of innocence. Unlike the other characters who are molded by their environments, he remains untouched by Fagin's world. This is not true because of any active volition on Oliver's part; Oliver wills to live and resists violently all of the attempts of the world to crush him, but one always has the sense that at the center of this strong will there is a passivity. Oliver wants to be rescued from Fagin and transported to a secure haven of refuge. One has difficulty picturing him seizing a place for himself in the world.

Critics sometime suggest that is logical that he has no character because he has no physical individuality, representing only the child element in a nightmare peopled by animals. His vision is Dicken's focus - world as seen through the fantasy fears and imagination of a child.

Dickens was one of the first writers to use a child as the hero of a novel. Unfortunately, however, Oliver is merely a puppet.

For all practical purposes, this is a novel without a hero. The force of evil in *Oliver Twist* is therefore much more vital and overpowering than the "passive" good which Oliver represents. Fagin is memorable; Oliver is merely remembered.

FAGIN

An ugly old Jew and a fence who also trains young boys to be pickpockets. In league with Oliver's half-brother Monks, he attempts unsuccessfully to make Oliver into a criminal. He is later caught and hanged. One of the most colorful villains in fiction, Fagin has life, imagination and cleverness. He is so captivating that we often forget his bestiality. We are less impressed with his eventual punishment than with the sheer force of his personality. Fagin represents the "Dickensian character" par excellence. His portrayal comes very close to caricature.

NANCY

A young prostitute who lives with Bill Sikes. Although she loves Sikes and is afraid of the gang, she protects Oliver from them. She is finally murdered by Sikes when Fagin informs him of her betrayal. It is her murder which eventually destroys Fagin's gang. Nancy is described as the "soul of goodness in things evil." She is the product of a nightmare society of endless drudgery. Her loyalty to Sikes seems inexplicable, until one remembers that he was the center of Nancy's world - a world in which natural affections were warped. Sikes gave her the feeling of womanliness, which she clung to even at the risk of her own life. She shared much of Rose's essential goodness; Dickens implies that she might have been like Rose in a different environment.

THE ARTFUL DODGER (JACK DAWKINS)

A strangely dressed boy pickpocket who befriends Oliver and introduces him to Fagin. "He was a snub-nosed, flat browed, common faced boy enough, ... but he had about him all the airs and manners of a man." Always asking questions which he answers himself, he is eventually sentenced to prison for stealing a silver snuff box.

BARNEY

The Jewish waiter at the Three Cripples. "Younger than Fagin, but nearly as vile and repulsive in appearance," his words "made their way through his nose." He helps Fagin and Toby during the burglary at Mrs. Maylie's.

CHARLEY BATES

Another youthful member of Fagin's gang who calls for help when Sikes attempts to hide in the warehouse. Appalled by Sikes' crime, he eventually becomes "the merriest grazier in all Northampton."

MRS. BEDWIN

Mr. Brownlow's kindly housekeeper who nurses Oliver back to health when Mr. Brownlow brings him home following the incident with Mr. Fang, the magistrate.

BET (BETSY)

A friend of Nancy, and the girlfriend of Tom Chitling. It is she who discovered Nancy's body after Sikes had murdered her.

BLATHERS

One of the Bow Street detectives who investigates the burglary at Mrs. Maylie's house. He represents Dickens' caricature of a London detective. For a more comprehensive portrait see Inspector Bucket in *Bleak House*.

BRITTLES

One of Mrs. Maylie's servants, a boy somewhat over thirty, who takes credit (with Giles) for the capture of the "dangerous" Oliver following the burglary.

MR. BROWNLOW

A kindly old gentleman who rescues Oliver from the "justice" of Mr. Fang. He later turns out to have been an old friend of Oliver's father; at the end of the story he adopts Oliver.

BULL'S-EYE

Sikes' shaggy, scarred dog, who like this master is savage, but cowardly. Because he follows Sikes everywhere, he eventually leads the police to Sikes' hiding place in the warehouse after Sikes murders Nancy. Fittingly, he dies with his master.

MR. BUMBLE

Aptly described by his name he is the fat beadle of the parish in which Oliver was born. Pompous, cruel, foolish, vain and greedy he marries Mrs. Corney and becomes master of the workhouse. They ironically end up as paupers in their own workhouse because of their involvement with Monks. Shorn of his authority, Bumble now becomes the object of the same callousness he had inflicted upon Oliver.

MRS. BUMBLE

(See Mrs. Corney)

CHARLOTTE

The ill-mannered servant girl of the Sowerberrys who, with Noah Claypole, mistreats Oliver. After stealing money from Mr. Sowerberry, she and Noah run away to London and become involved for a time with Fagin.

TOM CHITLING

A member of Fagin's gang, about eighteen, who has just been released from prison. He is a fervent admirer of the Artful Dodger and Toby Crackit, and later falls in love with Nancy's friend Betsy.

NOAH CLAYPOLE

A brutal, hulking, charity boy who like Oliver is apprenticed to Mr. Sowerberry. It is his mistreatment, as well as Charlotte's and Mrs. Sowerberry's, which causes Oliver to run away. Later he and Charlotte, who idolizes him, steal from Mr. Sowerberry and run away to London where Noah hopes to become a great "gentleman." Noah betrays Nancy to Fagin.

MRS. CORNEY

The matron of the workhouse where Oliver was born. She hides evidence of Oliver's parentage by concealing the pawn ticket for a locket and ring which she had gotten from the dying Old Sally. Later, married to Mr. Bumble, who is her male counterpart, she sells these articles to Monks who disposes of them. For their involvement with Monks, she and Mr. Bumble are discharged from their position and eventually become inmates of their own workhouse.

TOBY CRACKIT

Another burglar who with Bill Sikes participates in the attempted burglary at Mrs. Maylie's. Called "Flash" he is an older version of the Artful Dodger.

LITTLE DICK

A playmate, and friend of Oliver at the parish farm for children. It is he who gives Oliver his first blessing, but before Oliver can fulfill his promise and return for him, he dies of consumption brought on by starvation and Mrs. Mann's mistreatment.

DUFF

Another of the Bow Street detectives who with Blathers investigates the burglary at Mrs. Maylie's. He is a boney, sharp-eyed man with a "sinister looking nose." Like Blathers he represents another facet of Dickens' caricature of early London detectives.

MR. FANG

The police magistrate from whom Mr. Brownlow rescued Oliver when he was accused of stealing his handkerchief. A shouting, angry bully, he attempts to sentence Oliver without evidence until the weakened and hurt Olivers faints. He represents

Dickens' portrait of an actual magistrate, a Mr. Laing of Hatton Garden.

AGNES FLEMING

Oliver's mother, a young girl of nineteen, who die in the workhouse after giving birth to Oliver. The daughter of a retired naval officer, she gave birth to the child of Edwin Leeford unaware that he was married to Monks' mother, who swore to destroy all who knew the secret, and who forced her son, Monks, to continue that destruction after her death.

MR. GAMFIELD

The chimney sweep to whom Oliver is nearly apprenticed. Oliver is saved by a kindly magistrate who notes that Mr. Gamfield has already lost the lives of several previous apprentices.

GILES

Mrs. Maylie's butler, a foolish, cowardly man who shoots Oliver during the burglary, and later brags of his brave exploits before the women servants. He is, like Brittles, rather likeable in spite of his obvious faults.

MR. GRIMWIG

Mr. Brownlow's pessimistic friend. A gruff old bachelor, he reenforces the dogmatic arguments he makes by threatening to "eat my head." And although he at first is inclined to distrust Oliver, he later becomes his staunch friend.

KAGS

A returned transport (although sent to Australia for life, he has sneaked back) in whose hideout Sikes is at last caught.

EDWARD LEEFORD

(See Monks)

EDWIN LEEFORD

Although he never appears, he is important to the plot. He is the father of both Oliver and Monks, and it is his indiscretion which causes most of the mystery as well as the difficulty of the novel.

MV. LIMBKINS

A fat, red-faced gentleman who heads the parish board in the town where Oliver was born. The other members of the board are very much like him-callous and impersonal.

DR. LOSBERNE

A friend of the Maylies, he attends Oliver and protects him from the detectives, Blathers and Duff, after the burglary. He is a good-hearted but impulsive man who becomes one of Oliver's staunchest friends.

MRS. MANN

The matron at the farm where Oliver was reared. Grasping and greedy, she starves her charges for her own gain.

MRS. MAYLIE

A kindly, elderly widow who has adopted Rose from some local cottagers, and who befriends Oliver following the burglary at her home. Her son and Rose eventually marry.

HARRY MAYLIE

Mrs. Maylie's young son who gives up his budding career as a man of affairs, and a member of parliament, to become a clergyman and marry Rose.

ROSE MAYLIE

Mrs. Maylie's lovely seventeen-year-old ward. Believing herself to be illegimate as a result of rumors spread by Monks' mother, she refused to marry Harry Maylie. It is later discovered that she is not illegitimate; furthermore, she turns out to be the sister of Oliver's mother, Agnes.

MONKS (EDWARD LEEFORD)

Oliver's half-brother, son of Edwin Leeford. Under the influence of his mother and his own criminal nature, he plots to defraud Oliver of his rightful share of the fortune that their father left. Subject to epileptic fits, he is a nervous, unattractive man who returns to a life of crime after Oliver generously shares his inheritance with him.

OLD SALLY

The old midwife at the workhouse where Oliver was born. At her death, she confesses to Mrs. Corney that she had stolen a locket and a ring from Oliver's dying mother. Mrs. Corney later redeemed them from the pawnbrokers and sold them to Monks.

BILL SIKES

A crude, brutal thief involved with Fagin. Accompanied everywhere by his equally savage dog, Bull's-Eye, Sikes in a fit of rage murders Nancy, and is tracked down to a warehouse by a crowd which has followed his dog there. As he attempts to escape, he accidentally hangs himself.

MR. SOWERBERRY

A tall, gaunt, but not unkindly, undertaker to whom Oliver is apprenticed. Although he treats Oliver well, he is too afraid to interfere with his wife's mistreatment of the boy.

MRS. SOWERBERRY

An unattractive, shrewish, unpleasant woman who, allied with Noah and Charlotte, caused Oliver to run away from the undertaker's establishment.

OLIVER TWIST

CRITICAL COMMENTARY

From the beginning, Dickens' work has commanded the attention of critics who have, for the most part, been reduced to attempting to explain his enormous popularity in spite of numerous obvious flaws in the method of his work. Among the best of Dickens' early critics was Hypolite Taine, a famous French critic of English literature, and a contemporary of Dickens. For it was he who was among the first to note what later critics have come to recognize as flaws in Dickens' style, and to attempt to ascertain the reasons for the peculiar power of that style. "Consider," he wrote, "the imaginative power of Dickens, and you will perceive therein the cause of his faults and his merits, his power and his excess."

Most obvious of those faults which Taine discovered as inherent in Dickens' style was his "excessive imagination." This, of course, now something of a truism, is a necessary point of departure for any serious criticism of Dickens since his characters and scenes are often "larger than life" (Fagin, for example). Even "objects with Dickens take their hue from the thoughts of his characters." For example, when Oliver embarked on his journey from Mr. Sowerberry's the weather was cold and bleak, matching exactly Oliver's prospects. Note too that Sikes and Fagin are not merely criminals, but their manners, their attitudes, and their appearances are as ugly as their characters. Even more, the haunts of Fagin and Sikes are contrasted sharply with those of Mr. Brownlow or Mrs. Maylie. But we must remember that although Taine held this heightening of character and place as a flaw, he also argued that it was just as often the source of Dickens' power as a writer, since it helped him to satirize an oppressive social order.

Taine's criticism was expanded by G. K. Chesterton, who argued that Dickens was not a novelist at all, but a pure satirist; and defined the essence of Dickens' **satire** as an ability to perceive some "absurdity," and then to isolate "that absurdity so that all can see it." That there is some truth to this argument relative to *Oliver Twist* is, of course, obvious. Bumble, the beadle, is an example of brilliant satire-from his numerous malapropisms to his manner of dress. Dickens' criticism of the Poor Laws and the courts, though not so carefully or effectively directed as in *Bleak House* or *Hard Times*, nonetheless provided an effective as well as an essential background for his allegorical and melodramatic tale.

The charge of melodrama at the expense of "reality" has been brought against Dickens by numerous critics. It is, of course, one that can easily be substantiated, by Dickens' own admission. He used melodramatic techniques (drawn primarily from his experiences in the theater) quite self-consciously. *Oliver Twist* is in many respects a formula novel: the formula consisting of a skillful combination of melodrama with grotesque and humorous characterizations. Dickens alternated tragic and comic scenes to balance one against the other (and to tantalize an audience which was buying serial installments). He used all the tricks of his theater experience: coincidences, chance encounters, eavesdroppers, recognition scenes, guilty secrets, and stage effects. These techniques are considered "flaws" by modern critics, but they undoubtedly have lent *Oliver Twist* and other novels a vitality which still makes them popular today.

It is obvious to any knowledgeable reader of Dickens that *Oliver Twist* is a seminal novel. As modern critics like Edgar Johnson, Humphrey House, Monroe Engel, and A. J. O. Cockshut have made clear, Dickens' work if it is to be adequately evaluated must be viewed as a whole. And *Oliver Twist* is the first serious novel of an artist who grew in skill as he matured, of an artist who was seriously involved in the problems of his age.

Part of the difficulty in the criticism of Dickens' work is dependent upon whether or not the critic views that work as static and unchanging, or as work which underwent significant change. In addition each critic has had a tendency to view Dickens through the lens of his own prejudices, and through these to magnify or distort Dickens' faults or virtues in accordance with the critic's own tendencies. For example, Andre Maurois saw Dickens as a reflection of the optimistic philosophy of the English Victorian period. (There is something of this view in Taine as well). He argued that Dickens was always looking at the bright side of life because he felt because he felt that with a little kindness man could arrive at a "lasting Christmas." This view also seems essentially that of Stephan Zweig, who argued that Dickens "did not write as a free artist, but ... as an Anglican citizen."

Even in *Oliver Twist* the weakness of these criticisms must be apparent. For although the novel has a fairy tale quality, as a kind of allegory of good and evil, the novel cannot be said to look only at the bright side of life. Indeed, Dickens was one of the first to look realistically at the dark side. What made him different from the French realists was his unwillingness to sacrifice the imaginative possibilities of literature for those scientific theories of art which argued that the artist is merely a recorder and not a creator. For Dickens like most of his great contemporaries-Thackeray, Trollope, and George Eliot-left his personal imprint upon everything he wrote. And although he was critical of his age, he was not like the modern writer alienated from the society about which he wrote.

In the Preface to *Oliver Twist* Dickens declared that he intended to describe "a knot of such associates in crime as really do exist; to paint them in all their deformity, in all their wretchedness, in all the squalid poverty of their lives; to show them as they really are, for ever skulking uneasily through the dirtiest paths of life, with the great, black, ghastly gallows closing up their prospect." There were limitations to this "reality" which Dickens tried to portray. Certainly the reality of Fagin's world is more accurately portrayed (in the sense of "reported") than the world of Rose Maylie. Her world is rendered rather sentimentally and unconvincingly by Dickens.

At the same time that Dickens was trying to counteract the romantic view of the criminal world (for example, in the Newgate novels of the 1830s), he glossed over many of the more brutal aspects of Fagin's world. His dislike of too realistic detail is particularly apparent in the area of sexual life. Dickens never hints, as Humphrey House has pointed out, at the fact that the atmosphere of Fagin's den must have been "drenched in sex." Women like Nancy who were used to entrap young men into haunts like Fagin's certainly made use of every form of seductiveness.

In addition, Mr. House has also pointed out how Dickens, in describing the underworld, never defines precisely its more repugnant objects. "Dirt" is a word that recurs frequently in Dickens' descriptions of London, which do not go beyond generic terms of this kind. Mr. House describes this Victorian prudery as an aspect of the morality of the middle class, which Dickens accepted implicitly. Even though Dickens himself was separated from his wife and kept a mistress (not revealed until 1945), he was suffering from both the Victorian **conventions** about sex and a personal conflict about morality. Perhaps he did not wish to be too frank because he himself provided a typical case of Victorian hypocrisy.

The views of Maurois and Zweig were in part echoed by George Orwell, who approved Dickens' sympathetic attitude toward the poor but found his social criticism too general and lacking in constructive suggestions. "His whole message is ... if man would behave decently, the world would be decent." These criticisms, like the view of T. A. Jackson (who attempted to prove that Dickens was a Marxist), appear the result of critical viewpoints which are too limited, for they fail to adequately explain the reasons for Dickens' continuing popularity with all classes of readers. More sympathetic critics like Oliver Elton, Elizabeth Bowen, and George Gissing have generally agreed that Dickens was more of a realist than he has often been given credit for being.

For in *Oliver Twist*, though obviously Oliver is an artificial, two-dimensional character who strangely takes none of his character from his surroundings, other characters like Nancy, Sikes, and to some extent Fagin, are not the totally exaggerated caricatures they seem. They reveal instead Dickens' knowledge of the devices by which the underdog lived. There can be no doubt that any valid criticism of Dickens' work must take into account a thorough knowledge of Dickens' life and of the age in which he lived.

It is, however, true that most of Dickens' characters are created from the outside. That is, the reader is never permitted to see the inner workings of their minds and to discover exactly why they do what they do. As Edmund Wilsoni has pointed out, Dickens was "unable to get the good and the bad together in one character," with the result that the bad as well as the good characters seem to exist without adequate motivation. But, of course, Dickens did not feel it necessary to reveal the inner conflict or motivations of his characters. For him, and for the Victorian reader, the exterior view was enough. Moreover, Dickens' readers accepted willingly his omniscient view of his characters, for the Victorian reader knew what good and evil were. He knew the difference between greed and generosity, kindness and cruelty, and innocence and vice.

It is also true that in Dickens' day it was customary for the author of a novel to add, in his own voice either as narrator, or as an external commentator, a running commentary upon the action, the characters, and even the places in his novels. For example, in **Chapter Thirty-eight**, Dickens is not merely content to describe Monks' hideout, but is constrained to offer a comment upon it. "This was far from being a place of doubtful character, for it had long been known as a residence of none but low ruffians ... who subsisted chiefly on plunder and crime." Thus Dickens was not content to allow the reader to draw his own conclusions from the description, but made certain that he would draw the conclusions the author wished.

In his own way, then, Dickens in *Oliver Twist*, as he was always to do, gave an objective exterior view of life, modified by his own moral and ethical precepts. And he did more than merely reflect the attitudes of his age, he helped to shape them. Thus, although an examination of Dickens' work reveals deficiencies of style, his use of caricature, his addition of melodrama, his artificialities and **conventions** of plot, and his inability to portray accurately certain types of characters (almost nowhere does Dickens attempt successfully the upper classes); that examination also reveals that Dickens was great enough to transcend these deficiencies. And finally what emerges from that examination is a portrait of a fantastically successful literary artist, whose imagination wonderfully transformed the material of his experience, and revealed his love of humanity.

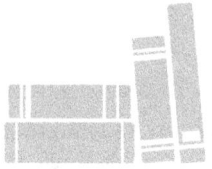

OLIVER TWIST

ESSAY QUESTIONS AND ANSWERS

Question: What are some of the injustices which Dickens attacks in the course of *Oliver Twist*?

Answer: The major targets of Dickens' **satire** are the Poor Laws which represent an attempt to discourage poverty by dividing families and placing them in workhouses where they are worked as hard and fed as little as possible. He is also critical of those greedy and incompetent petty officials and muddle-headed board members whose function is to administer those institutions.

A second target of Dickens' **satire** is that form of justice represented by Mr. Fang, a cruel and incompetent judge who unjustly sentences Oliver without allowing him a proper defense. Dickens continues this attack with his humorous description of the work of the Bow Street runners, Blathers and Duff, whose investigation of the burglary at Mrs. Maylie's is thwarted by Dr. Losberne.

A third, and not so clearly defined criticism of Dickens' in *Oliver Twist*, is of that governmental and economic system which causes such widespread poverty, desolation, and the crime which it produces. His description of the slums of Saffron Hill, and Jacob's Island, as well as his description of the poor who inhabit them constitute perhaps his strongest criticism. For as Nancy tells us, people like her, and the Dodger and Charley Bates are forced into crime if they wish to exist. Dickens also attacked the complacent frame of mind which allowed such abuses to continue to be ignored.

Question: What are some of the techniques by which Dickens creates characters in *Oliver Twist*?

Answer: Dickens creates his characters in many ways. First, a character's personality may be noted by the way in which he is described. For example, the evil and ugly appearances of such characters as Fagin, Sikes, and Monks are due to their character. The same, of course, is true of the novel's good characters. For Oliver, Rose, and Mr. Brownlow are attractive characters. Second, a character may be revealed by his manner of speech. Mr. Grimwig's "I'll eat my head" reveals his stubbornness, and Mr. Bumble's perpetually speaking of his "parochial duties" reveals his inflated sense of his own importance.

In addition to these Dickens employs the more usual means of creating characters. Often speaking in his own person as a narrator, he tells us what characters are like, or he tells us of the actions they undertake. By the manner in which he describes them we approve or disapprove. For example, when Monks and Fagin meet furtively at the dirty, disreputable Three Cripples tavern, we do not know what they plan, but we do know they are plotting nothing good. And in the same manner we know Mr. Brownlow to be a good man when he kindly defends Oliver before Mr. Fang, and then carries him home to care for him.

Question: What elements of melodrama are obvious in the plot of *Oliver Twist*?

Answer: It is obvious that most of the plot of *Oliver Twist* is arranged for the convenience of the author. For example, when Oliver is rescued by Mr. Brownlow from the magistrate, although Oliver does not know it, Mr. Brownlow is an old friend of his father, and the portrait which hangs on a wall at Mr. Brownlow's is of Oliver's mother. Nor is this the only coincidence in the novel, for when Oliver is rescued a second time by the Maylies, Rose Maylie later proves to be his mother's younger sister. And late in the novel, Noah and Charlotte just happen to meet Fagin at the Three Cripples tavern on their first evening in London.

In addition the novel contains many chance meetings. For example, Monks' arrangements with Fagin, we are told, are the result of Monks' accidentally seeing Oliver with Fagin's pupils early in the story. And later in the novel, Monks again discovers Oliver's whereabouts when he accidentally sees Oliver in the carriage with Dr. Losberne. Moreover, many of the novel's scenes are melodramatic, either too theatrical or too heavily laden with poetic justice. Good examples, of course, are the descriptions of the burglary at the Maylies' and the ensuing flight, and the death of Sikes as he attempted to flee the crowd over the rooftops.

Question: What plot weaknesses are probably the result of serial publication?

Answer: Written in monthly installments, each of which ends with a climactic moment to whet the reader's appetite for the next issue, the plot of *Oliver Twist* contains a number of awkward breaks. For example, although we are told that Monks and Sikes had sealed their bargain about what to do with Oliver early in the story, nowhere does Monks appear in that portion of the narrative where that bargain was supposed to have been made. Then, too, some of the plot's many climaxes are contrived, as for example in the case of Rose's illness, following as it does Oliver's second. Each of these confinements does little to advance the plot, but serves only to leave the serial reader "cliff-hanging" until the next issue. Nor is the plot made more coherent by the frequent switches from one portion of the narrative to another. When we are told Oliver has been wounded in **Chapter Twenty-two**, we must wait until **Chapter Twenty-eight** before we discover what happens to him next. And although Mr. Bumble's and Mrs. Corney's interest in one another is revealed in **Chapter Twenty-three**, we must wait until **Chapter Thirty-seven** before we discover that they have married.

Question: How well does Dickens portray middle - and lower-class characters in *Oliver Twist*?

Answer: Although Dickens obviously knew the middle-class well, since as a reporter and editor he was a part of that class, these characters do not emerge as fully recognizable portraits in *Oliver Twist*. For such characters as Mr. Brownlow, Mr. Grimwig, Dr. Losberne, and the Maylies are never detailed. Instead they are drawn sketchily as characters who are good, but indistinct. Those of the lower classes in *Oliver Twist*, however, do emerge as fully drawn figures. Although Fagin, Sikes, and Mr. Bumble are often caricatures, they are believable. Moreover, based on Dickens' knowledge of the London underworld, they are, in addition, characters who could have existed, according to the accounts of Dicken's contemporaries.

Question: Who are some of the humorous characters of *Oliver Twist* and what about them accounts for their humor?

Answer: Although *Oliver Twist* is a novel far more serious than *Pickwick Papers*, it is not a novel totally devoid of Dickensian humor. Such characters as Giles and Brittles, the humorous portraits of the Bow Street detectives, and the humorous aspects of such diverse characters as the Artful Dodger, Charley Bates, Tom Chitling, and Barney do much to relieve the novel's somber aspects. For Giles and Brittles are the theatrical counterparts of the talkative and humorous servants of the Elizabethan and Restoration stage. Although they talk bravely, their cowardice is obvious. What, of course, saves them from being merely ridiculous is the fact that their loyalties and their motives are good. Nor can we for long take the Bow Street detectives seriously, for their foreboding appearance is almost instantly belied by their obvious incompetence.

Nor are some of the novel's more serious participants entirely lacking in humor. Even though they are thieves, we cannot help but be amused by the humorous antics and dress of Fagin, the Dodger, Charley Bates, and of Tom Chitling's chuckleheaded admiration of "Flash" Toby Crackit. And though Barney's tendency to speak through his nose requires some effort to understand what he says, we cannot help but smile appreciatively at Dickens' phonetic inventiveness.

Question: How is atmosphere used in *Oliver Twist*?

Answer: Dickens' use of atmosphere in *Oliver Twist* does more than merely provide appropriate background for the story. For not only does Dickens use background to reveal character - as in the case of Monks who had epileptic fits brought on by thunderstorms, or Sikes whose enterprises seem perpetually surrounded by gloomy and rainy weather - but background is often a **foreshadowing** of events to come. For example, Nancy's furtive meetings with Rose and Mr. Brownlow take place on the foggy London Bridge over the dark and foreboding Thames where Nancy's premonition of death is in part inspired by the gloomy scene.

By contrast the scenes of Oliver's happier days at Mr. Brownlow's, and Mrs. Maylie's seem perpetually bathed in sunshine. Note for example that when Oliver leaves on his errand for Mr. Brownlow, it is nearly night, and he is kidnapped by Nancy and Sikes just as the daylight fades. So too have Oliver's fortunes changed from daylight to darkness. And although the haunts of the novel's evil characters may seem merely appropriate to their social status, those haunts are more than simply old and dilapidated buildings. Rather they seem to acquire some of the evil atmosphere from their inhabitants.

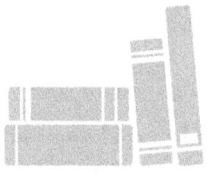

BIBLIOGRAPHY

The following is a highly selective list of some of the most important criticisms of *Oliver Twist* and of Dickens' work, arranged alphabetically by author within key research topics.

BIOGRAPHIC STUDIES

Forster, John. *The Life of Charles Dickens*. Ed. by J. W. T. Ley, London: *Dent*, 1928. Also available as paperback in E. P. Dutton Everyman Library Edition, 2 vol. By Dickens' lifelong friend, this has long been the standard biography.

Johnson, Edgar. *Charles Dickens: His Tragedy and Triumph*. 2 vols., New York: *Simon & Shuster*, 1952. Excellent modern biography, more comprehensive than Forster.

Leacock, Stephen B. *Charles Dickens: His Life and Work*. New York: *Doubleday*, 1934. A short, readable biography, excellent for younger students.

Pearson, Hesketh. *Dickens: His Character, Comedy, and Career*. New York: *Harper Bros.*, 1949. An interesting popular biography. Very readable.

DICKENS AND HIS SOURCES

Questions to consider:

What were some of Dickens' sources for *Oliver Twist*?

How much of *Oliver Twist* is autobiographical?

How did Dickens transform the material of his experience?

The primary sources, of course, for answers to these questions can be found in the biographies.

Collins, Phillip. *Dickens and Crime*. London: Macmillan, 1962.

Holdsworth, Sir William. *Charles Dickens as Legal Historian*. Hew Haven: Yale, 1929.

Van Amerongen, J. B. *The Actor in Dickens*. New York: Appleton Century, 1927.

Wilson, Edmund. "The Two Scrooges," *The Wound and the Bow*. Boston, 1941. A valuable study of the effect of Dickens' early experiences on his work.

DICKENS AND HIS METHOD

Questions to consider:

How did Dickens create his characters?

How accurate are Dickens' portraits of the various classes of society?

Who are Dickens "grotesques"?

Do they represent accurate portrayals?

Does Dickens' style undergo any significant change in his later novels?

How much of Dickens' theatrical experience influences his work as a novelist?

How successful were Dickens' theatrical ventures?

Butt, John and Kathleen Tillotson. *Dickens at Work. Fairlawn, N. J.: Essential Books*, 1958. A valuable guide containing the notes for all of Dickens' novels.

Chesterton, G. K. *Criticism and Appreciation of the Works of Charles Dickens.* London: Dent, 1933.

Cockshut, A. O. J. *The Imagination of Charles Dickens.* New York: *N. Y. U. Press*, 1962. An excellent discussion of Dickens' use of symbols and of his changing views as a novelist. Includes discussions of all Dickens' major novels.

Engel, Monroe. *The Maturity of Charles Dickens.* Cambridge, Mass.: Harvard Univ. Press, 1959. Excellent discussion of Dickens' growth as a novelist.

Fawcett, F. D. *Dickens the Dramatist.* London: *W. H. Allen*, 1952. (By S. Stokes, pseud.) Good discussion of Dickens' lifelong interest in the theater.

Ford, George H. *Dickens and His Readers.* Princeton: Princeton U. Press, 1955.

Woolcott, Alexander. *Mr. Dickens Goes to the Play.* New York: *Putnam*, 1922. A witty discussion of Dickens' interest in the theater.

DICKENS AND HIS AGE

Questions to consider:

What does Dickens' criticism of crime and poverty reveal about his own attitudes?

Does Dickens' attitude change in his later work?

How good a recorder of his age was Dickens?

How much influence did Dickens have in changing the attitudes and institutions of the Victorian age?

Christie, O. F. *Dickens and His Age*. London: *Heath, Cranton*, 1939.

Dexter, Walter. *The England of Dickens*. Phila.: *Lippincott*, 1925. Good general discussion of that portion of the Victorian age about which Dickens wrote.

Gissing, George R. *Critical Studies of the Works of Charles Dickens*. New York: *Greenberg*, 1924. Among the most perceptive of the early criticisms.

House, Humphry. *The Dickens World*. London: Oxford, 1941. A detailed study of the historical settings of Dickens' novels.

Miller, J. Hillis. *Charles Dickens: The World of His Novels*. Cambridge, Mass.: Harvard Univ. Press, 1958. Good discussion of Oliver Twist.

DICKENS AND HIS CONTEMPORARIES

Questions to consider:

What were Dickens' relations with the other great Victorian novelists?

Who were some of Dickens' friends and how was he influenced by them?

What is Dickens' place in the history of the English novel?

Allen, Walter. *The English Novel.* New York: *Dutton*, 1954, pp. 179-198. A good, short history of the English novel.

The pages indicated refer to Allen's discussion of Dickens and his place in that history.

Baily, Francis. Six Great-Victorian Novelists. *London:* MacDonald, *1947.*

Cecil, Lord David. *The Early Victorian Novelists.* New York: *Bobbs-Merrill,* 1935. Good, readable comparative study, discusses Dickens as part of Victorian mainstream.

Fielding, K. J. *Charles Dickens: A Critical Introduction.* London: *Longmans, Green & Co.* 1958. An informative discussion of the relation of Dickens' work to his life.

Quiller-Couch, Sir Arthur. *Charles Dickens and Other Victorians.* London: Cambridge, 1925.

Stevenson, Lionel (Ed.). *Victorian Fiction: A Guide to Research.* Cambridge: *Harvard,* 1964. Contains an excellent summary of Dickens' criticism.

Tillotson, Kathleen. *Novels of the Eighteen-Forties.* London: Oxford, 1954. Contains valuable discussion of *Oliver Twist.*

Wagenknecht, Edward. *The Cavalcade of the English Novel.* New York: *Holt, Rinehart & Winston,* 1954, pp. 213-233. Contains good bibliography.

GENERAL CRITICISM AND FURTHER BIBLIOGRAPHIC SOURCES

The Dickensian. Published monthly 1905-1918; Quarterly 1919-__. Vols. I-XLVII. A periodical devoted entirely to articles and studies on Dickens.

Cambridge Bibliography of English Literature III, *pp. 435-455. See also supplementary Vol. V.*

P.M.L.A. (Annual bibliography in May issues). Since 1956 has included articles by both English and American scholars.

Trevelyan, G. M. *Illustrated English Social History.* Vol. IV. New York: *Longmans Green & Co.*, 1952. Readable interesting history of England in Dickens' day.

"Victorian Bibliography," annually in *Modern Philology*, 1933-57, and *Victorian Studies*, 1958-__.

Young, G. M. (Ed.) *Early Victorian England 1830-1865.* 2 Vols., London: *Oxford*, 1934.

SUGGESTIONS FOR RESEARCH PAPER TOPICS

Smollett's influence of Dickens, as seen in *Oliver Twist.*

Dickens' view of Victorian economic system.

Oliver Twist as a fairy tale.

Dickens as a social critic in *Oliver Twist.*

The structure of *Oliver Twist*, as influenced by serial publication.

Symbols and **imagery** in *Oliver Twist*.

Oliver's moral choice.

Dickens' comic characterization through dialogue: Mr. Bumble, Giles & Brittles, etc.

Dickens' preoccupation with crime and criminals.

Dickens' understanding of the child's mind and imagination.

Dickens' estimate of Victorian "Society" in *Oliver Twist*.

Dickens as a satirist.

Use of **irony** and **parody** in *Oliver Twist*.

Dickens' view of the courts, as seen in *Oliver Twist*.

Oliver Twist as an attack on the Poor Laws.

The critics and *Oliver Twist*.

Autobiographical material in *Oliver Twist*.

The significance of *Oliver Twist* for our time.

EXPLORE THE ENTIRE LIBRARY OF BRIGHT NOTES STUDY GUIDES

From Shakespeare to Sinclair Lewis and from Plato to Pearl S. Buck, The Bright Notes Study Guide library spans hundreds of volumes, providing clear and comprehensive insights into the world's greatest literature. Discover more, faster with the Bright Notes Study Guide to the classics you're reading today.

See the entire library of available
Bright Notes guides at **BrightNotes.com**

Available in print and digital wherever books are sold

IP INFLUENCE PUBLISHERS

www.ingramcontent.com/pod-product-compliance
Lightning Source LLC
LaVergne TN
LVHW011721060526
838200LV00051B/2990